The Multi Cooker Book

The Multi Cooker Book

Recipes for the Electric Frying Pan

by
HELEN M. COX

FABER AND FABER
London · Boston

First published in 1980
by Faber and Faber Limited
3 Queen Square London WC1N 3AU
Printed in Great Britain by
Latimer Trend & Company Ltd Plymouth
All rights reserved

British Library Cataloguing in Publication Data

Cox, Helen M.
   The multi cooker book
   1. Electric cookery
   I. Title
   641.5'88   TX827

   ISBN 0-571-11474-1
   ISBN 0-571-11475-x Pbk

Contents

The Multi Cooker

'Since I have had my Multi Cooker,' wrote an enthusiastic friend, 'I have seldom used my oven. I save on electricity bills and can roast a chicken, make a cake and do successful long slow cooking.' Many other owners of Multi Cookers would endorse this.

Electric frypan, automatic frypan or automatic cooker were the names once given to the Cooker, but because its use extends far beyond just frying it is now more appropriately called the Multi Cooker.

This book is related directly to the Sunbeam Multi Cooker but owners of other makes will find the recipes equally useful. Many recipes have been written for just two servings, others for larger families, and some dishes for special occasions have also been included.

The Multi Cooker can be used for:

Roasting chicken and other meats.
Baking cakes, bread, puddings and pies.
Frying fish, steaks, chops, sausages, bacon, eggs, etc.
Braising and stewing meats, poultry and vegetarian dishes.
Boiling rice and pasta dishes, meats and poultry.
Casseroling foods cooked inside a casserole inside the Cooker.
Steaming foods cooked on the rack above simmering water.

In addition it can be used as:

A bain-marie—for cooking several different foods, in dishes standing in boiling water.

7

A slow cooker—for low heating of casseroled foods, allowing up to 10 hours' cooking.

A double-boiler—for cooking custards and other egg dishes which must not be boiled.

Slow-cooking crock

This is a large, thick, lidless dish (the Cooker cover alone is used) which fits exactly into the Cooker and may be purchased as an optional extra. It has only become available since this book was written, but the slow-cooking recipes can all be used with the same temperatures and timing. Because of the large area of its base, the crock is more suitable for 4 or more servings than for smaller quantities, but larger amounts could be cooked and the surplus stored in the deep-freeze.

As the crock is made of thick pottery, and so heats slowly, any preliminary frying should be done either in the Cooker or a separate pan. The crock can also be used for the faster-cooking recipes, especially cook-and-serve dishes. Less liquid is needed as it does not boil off as quickly.

The newer Multi Cooker models have some design improvements.

1 The thermostat may be pulled out, and the Cooker taken straight to the table, or to the sink for washing.
2 Covers are now fitted with a hinge-ratchet which fits into the handle and will hold the cover up at a choice of 3 angles. See p. 14 for using the lid as a splashback.
3 The insides of some Cookers have a non-stick finish and many exteriors are painted in bright, attractive colours.

How fuel costs are saved

1 When the Multi Cooker is being used for roasting or baking, the heat needed to bring it to the required temperature is *far less* than that needed for the oven of a gas or electric stove, which has a greater area and surface to heat. Only when conventional ovens are filled to capacity can they be said to compete.
2 This economy of fuel is continued during the cooking. In some recipes, because of the lower temperature overall, a little more time is needed, but the fuel saving is still considerable.

The Multi Cooker has this further advantage over the larger

8

stoves: heat is not retained and wasted after the cooking is finished, and at the beginning the required temperature is soon reached.

No-oven kitchens: Many small kitchens cannot accommodate conventional gas or electric stoves with their hobs and ovens, but with a Multi Cooker heading the kitchen equipment the larger stoves will not be missed. If you have in addition a grilling oven and hot plate, and possibly a small-sized pressure cooker, practically the entire culinary range is at your disposal.

Light weight: An advantage for those who hate heavy kitchen equipment (and I am one) is that the Multi Cooker, considering its size and strong construction, is surprisingly light.

CARE AND USE

Always keep the Multi Cooker in a handy position, ready for use at all times. If it is put away in a cupboard, the tendency is to put off bringing it out, while if it is there on your kitchen work-top, you will not be able to resist using it constantly.

A level surface: It is important that the surface on which the Multi Cooker stands is level. This will prevent fat and gravy from running to one end and cooking unevenly. If your work-top is uneven, put a little piece of wood under two of the Cooker legs to raise the Cooker to a level position.

Seasoning the surface of the Cooker: Whether your pan has a non-stick surface or not, it is a good idea to season it before use. Brush over the inside surface with oil and turn the heat on at 420 (6). As soon as the Cooker light goes out turn the heat off. This will improve the non-stick quality and helps prevent sticking in the untreated pans. Some people recommend sprinkling over the oil with salt before heating; any salty residue can be wiped off when the Cooker is cool.

Care of Teflon 2 cooking surface: Avoid cutting into the surface with sharp kitchen knives or other sharp implements. Fine scratches will not harm the non-stick qualities, but will affect the smooth appearance.

9

Temperatures: The numbers given in the recipes indicate the heat to which the thermometer will register. These are subject to slight variations in the different types or ages of Cookers, but they can be taken as a good general guide. They are not meant to be exact Fahrenheit or Centigrade readings, but to indicate the grading of heats from the maximum down to the lowest.

The latest Multi Cooker models have changed to single numbers from 1 (lowest) to 6 (highest); in the recipes these have been put beside the numbers used in previous models.

Some makes of Cooker use Centigrade numbers. The following table provides the necessary conversions.

200° C is about equal to Multi Cooker 420 or 6
175° C is between Multi Cooker 380 or 5 and Multi Cooker 340 or 4
150° C is about equal to Multi Cooker 300 or 3
125° C is about equal to Multi Cooker 260 or 2
100° C is about equal to Multi Cooker 220 or 1

After a number of years of constant use, the thermostat sometimes registers inaccurately and the Cooker may not give sufficient heat for cakes or pastry. If this happens, it may be advisable to have the thermostat control repaired or replaced.

Safety: Remember that the outside of the Cooker and the lid will be hot (like any saucepans and frying pans in use), so be careful not to let your plastic jugs or bowls lean against the Cooker when it is on. I mention this from experience.

Caution: the cover must never be used when deep-frying.

The rack: A baking-rack is essential if you are to make full use of your Cooker. It should be 9 in (23 cm) square and ¼–½ in (0·5–1·25 cm) high. In addition, a smaller 6–6½ in (16 cm) rack is very useful when roasting. Potatoes are placed around the rack in the fat.

The vent: Whether this is open or closed is important to the cooking. The instruction is with each recipe.

Directions for using the Multi Cooker or any electric frypan
1 Always put the fat or cold water into the Cooker before turning on the heat.

2 According to the instructions in the recipes, turn the knob to the suggested number. The heat may vary a little from one pan to another, but you will soon learn to judge your own and adjust accordingly. For instance, a good frying temperature might be exactly 340 (4) in your Cooker, but a fraction more or less in another.

3 To bring water to the boil, put in the water first, then turn to 220 (1). The heat will stay full on until the light goes out. It is no help to use a higher number to speed things up.

4 Never put cold water into the Cooker while it is very hot. To wash without having to bring it to the sink, put in a pint of water and a little washing-up liquid and bring to the boil. Turn off heat and clean with a brush.

5 If it is necessary to wash the Cooker in the sink, first switch off the power and remove power plug. Disconnect the removable thermostat control: it must not get wet. After washing the pan make sure the socket and pins are dry. The thermostat controls of some older models are built in and it is most important that they should not be immersed in water.

As a warmer: For late homecomers, a meal may be kept hot and moist in the Multi Cooker. Simmer a little water in the Cooker and put in the rack. Place the plate of food on the rack, covered with either another plate or foil. Cover with Cooker lid and close vent. Have thermostat well below 220 (1). Add more water if the time goes on and it evaporates (with your patience!).

Rolls and scones may be heated just by putting them on the hot lid while the Cooker is in use. But if they have become stale and need a lot of restoration, put them on the rack (when Cooker is empty), turn heat to 420 (6), cover with lid and close vent. In about 5–8 minutes they will be as soft and fresh as new. For thawing deep-frozen rolls see p. 162.

To freshen stale bread, wrap it in foil and place on rack in the Cooker. Cover with lid and open vent. Turn heat to 420 (6) and leave for 15–20 minutes, depending on the size of the loaf. For thawing deep-frozen bread see p. 162.

Warming dishes. When the meal is being cooked in a pressure cooker or other appliance, the Multi Cooker may be used as a warmer for the dishes. It will warm plates, a serving dish and soup bowls at one time. The soup bowls may be placed either on the lid, upside-down over the knob, or inside the serving dish. Have the lid on, vent open, and heat down to Simmer or below. Use the rack.

Lid heat: While the Cooker is in use, the lid heat can be used in many ways: to dry cake tins before they are put away; to dry a tea towel or dishcloth; to keep toast warm in the toast-rack or, if you are working close at hand, to keep a cup of tea or coffee warm between sips.

Using the lid as a splashback: Most of the up-to-date models have lids that will stay up in three positions. The lid can therefore be used as a splashback to prevent fat from splashing on to the wall when frying fast or in deep fat. With normal frying at a moderate temperature, splashing should not take place.

Extension lead: If you wish to carry the Cooker to the table and keep the contents hot (with a fondue, for instance) buy an extension lead that will reach to the nearest electric point.

COOKING HINTS

Thickening: When using the Cooker as a 'cook-and-serve dish' the thickening should not be added at the beginning, as in casseroling. Last-minute thickening may be done in three ways. (1) The usual way of mixing flour with cold water until smooth, then stirring in until thickened; (2) using packet soup-mix of any flavour you choose; (3) using your own homemade roux (*see below*). The last two methods have the advantage of ensuring that the flour has been well cooked previously, so that no taste of half-cooked flour will spoil the flavour of the dish. Packet soup-mix can be quite salty, so if using this method of thickening be sparing with the addition of salt as seasoning during cooking.

Homemade roux: If you always keep this in your cupboard, you will find that it has many uses and will save a lot of time. Melt 4 oz (100 g) butter in a small saucepan and stir in 4 oz (100 g) plain flour. Cook gently, *without browning*, for 4 minutes. Store in a covered jar but do not keep in the refrigerator; the roux will become too hard to use easily. The 4-minute cooking of the butter and flour ensures that it will keep for six or more weeks in a normally cool cupboard. Use 1 rounded tablespoon roux to thicken about ½ pint (275 ml) milk for a sauce; and use in the same proportion for thickening gravies or soups. If the liquid is not thick enough, extra roux can easily be added.

To crush garlic: Place the clove on a board and cut into 2 or 3 pieces. Crush then with the flat blade of a knife. A little salt helps.

To soften butter: Put butter on a plate. Pour boiling or very hot water into a heatproof bowl. When the bowl is thoroughly heated, pour out the water and up-end the bowl over the butter. It will soften the butter gently and evenly right through.

Peeling tomatoes: Put tomatoes into boiling or very hot water for a few minutes, then pour off the water and replace with cold to make handling easier. Peel off skins. If tomatoes are not needed for immediate use they can be put in the refrigerator with the skins on. They can then be peeled, when required, just as easily and they will be firmer. This is a help when slicing for salads or garnishes. Another method is to spear the tomato on the prongs of a fork and hold it over a gas jet, moving it around until skin loosens.

Oil for frying or for use in cakes, scones and biscuits: Corn oil, soya bean oil and other such cooking-oils are more suitable than lard or other cooking fats for semi-deep or deep frying. They splash less and providing they are not heated to excess, do not fill the kitchen with fumes. As an ingredient in certain cakes, or scones and biscuits, oil can be a time-saving substitute for butter or margarine.

Foil freezer containers: In a small kitchen there is not always cupboard space for an extensive range of cooking-pans. Foil containers are available in a variety of shapes and sizes and can be used for pies, cakes and bread.

MEASUREMENTS

In former days when Bristish cooking was at its best, measurdments were surprisingly haphazard. Quantities were given in cups, spoons and handfuls and the liquid had to be 'sufficient for a good consistency'. Today chefs still throw a pile of flour on the marble slab when about to make pastry, and pick up a bottle of wine and *pour* when making some delicious dish.

The metric equivalents given in recipes cannot be exact; they are approximate but always proportionate. *It is, therefore, important to stick to imperial or metric measurements within each recipe and not switch from one to the other.*

As cooking is not an *exact* science the metric measures have been rounded off in order to ease the transition in the kitchen. The finished quantity of some recipes may be slightly less where metric measures are used than with imperial. The following table is used here.

Weights
Kilogram is shown as kg. It is a little over 2 lb.
Gram is shown as g: a tiny quantity.
25 g may replace 1 oz.
100 g may replace 4 oz.
450 g may replace 1 lb which may be called $\frac{1}{2}$ kg.

Liquids
A litre is a little over $1\frac{3}{4}$ pints.
Millilitre is shown as ml and is one-thousandth of a litre.
150 ml may replace $\frac{1}{4}$ pint or 1 gill.
275 ml may replace $\frac{1}{2}$ pint.
575 ml may replace 1 pint.

Do not feel that the cooking has to stop when faced with measurements in the metric system. If you wished you could ignore it and return to the quick and simple methods of our ancestors. All you need is a cup that will hold $\frac{1}{2}$ pint of liquid and a set of measuring-spoons.

Here is a general table:

	Approx.
1 cup of liquid	$\frac{1}{2}$ pint or 10 fluid oz or $\frac{1}{4}$ litre
1 cup of flour	$5\frac{1}{2}$ oz or 163 g
1 cup of granulated sugar	8 oz or 225 g
1 cup of icing sugar	6 oz or 175 g
1 cup of rice	8 oz or 225 g
1 cup of sultanas	4 oz or 100 g
1 cup of breadcrumbs	2 oz or 50 g
1 level tablespoon butter	$\frac{1}{2}$ oz or 12·5 g
1 rounded tablespoon butter	1 oz or 25 g
1 rounded tablespoon sugar	1 oz or 25 g
$2\frac{1}{2}$ level tablespoons flour	1 oz or 25 g

Note: If you haven't a $\frac{1}{2}$ pint cup, use your measuring jug instead. It will have the usual $\frac{1}{4}$, $\frac{1}{2}$ and 1 pint lines and these could also be used for measuring solids. For instance, $5\frac{1}{2}$ oz of flour will come up to the $\frac{1}{2}$ pint line and so will 8 oz of sugar or rice. Your measuring spoons will deal with the odd measurements such as 3 oz, etc. Follow the table set out above.

American measurements

1 cup	8 fl oz liquid	All measurements level
1 cup	$4\frac{1}{2}$ oz flour or cornflour	
1 cup	7 oz rice	

1 tablespoon	$\frac{1}{2}$ oz flour	All measurements level
1 tablespoon	$\frac{3}{4}$ oz sugar	
1 tablespoon	$\frac{3}{4}$ oz butter	

Note: These American cups are equivalent in size to the new metric cups in Australia and New Zealand.

Recipes

1

Breakfast Dishes
Fish, Luncheon and Supper Dishes
Vegetarian and Vegetable Dishes
Cocktail Party Savouries

Quite a number of the recipes in this chapter have been designed for two people so these may be halved easily for one, giving ideas for those who live alone.

For fish-lovers there is an interesting variety of different types of dishes; and if you wish occasionally to replace meat with other proteins, the chapter includes dishes using pulses.

Vegetarians too have not been forgotten.

HOMEMADE MUESLI

as a toaster

Most firms selling foodstuffs, whether chain-stores or chemists, have their own mixtures and brand names for muesli. The idea for such a mixture originated in Switzerland and was called 'the Swiss breakfast'. Since then the variety of ingredients possible has increased and we can select the combination that we prefer.

4 oz (100 g) quick-cooking oats
2–3 oz (50–75 g) chopped walnuts, whole hazelnuts, peanuts, or a mixture
2 tablespoons wheatgerm
4 tablespoons bran
2 tablespoons ready-toasted buckwheat
1 or more tablespoons dark soft brown sugar

4 or more tablespoons sultanas or raisins, or a mixture
2 oz (50 g) dates, stoned and chopped
1 heaped tablespoon dried milk powder
¼ teaspoon salt
3 oz (75 g), or more, chopped dried tree fruits, such as apples, apricots, pears or peaches

1 Put oats and nuts into Cooker and turn heat to 380 (5).
2 After about 3 minutes they will begin to colour, so move them about with a spatula and toast until a light brown.
3 Tip into a bowl and stir in all the other ingredients.
4 When cold, store in a jar and cover with lid. Serve for breakfast with milk or yoghurt and/or fruit. Lots of goodness there to start the day!

Note: Other ingredients such as rolled oats, wheatflakes, grapenuts or desiccated coconut may be added or could replace some of the ingredients in the recipe. There is no hard and fast rule for muesli; a very good one could be made using only some of the ingredients listed.

HOMEMADE YOGHURT

as a yoghurt maker

Because the Cooker can maintain a low heat indefinitely, it is the perfect yoghurt maker. Homemade yoghurt can be enriched, sweetened and flavoured to suit your taste, and costs about one-quarter of the shop price. It is important to use utensils and containers that are clean so sterilize them by pouring boiling water over them before you begin.

MILK

1 pint (575 ml) long-life milk, or other sterilized milk; or 1 pint (575 ml) ordinary milk, brought almost to the boil then cooled to blood heat; or 5 heaped tablespoons dried milk with 1 pint (575 ml) cold water; or a 5 fl oz (150 ml) can evaporated milk, diluted with water to make ¾ pint (425 ml)

SWEETENING

sugar or saccharin tablets to taste, mixed into the milk; or honey, stirred in after the yoghurt has been made (1 tablespoon malted milk powder in place of some, or all, of the sugar will both enrich and sweeten the yoghurt)

FLAVOURING

chopped fresh fruit, dried fruits (soaked and chopped where necessary) and chopped nuts; cocoa or instant coffee (about 1 dessertspoon to 1 pint (575 ml) milk). Stir the flavouring into the yoghurt after it has been made and cooled.

YOGHURT STARTER

natural yoghurt is used for this and should be bought fresh (*see Note p. 21*). It should be firm, not runny. Use 1 scant tablespoon for 1 pint (575 ml) milk, less will give a blander taste. You can also use some of your own yoghurt as a starter

1 Put all but a small amount of the milk into a jug.
2 Pour the rest of the milk into a bowl. Add the sweetening, if liked. Add the yoghurt starter (keep the remainder of the carton for further batches of homemade yoghurt). Mix well.
3 Pour this into the jug of milk and stir.

4 Pour into cartons. Four cartons 4 in (10 cm) in diameter (margarine tubs, for instance) will take 1 pint (575 ml). Smaller cartons can be used (the same size as the bought natural yoghurt), with a variety of flavours. One carton could be left unflavoured to provide a starter for your next batch. This will work two or three times, but it will become runny, and a fresh carton should then be bought. Place cartons on rack in Cooker and cover with lid.

5 Have the indicator at the 'off' position. Move it up slowly and stop as soon as the light comes on. Leave it there. The light will come on at long intervals and keep the heat gentle and constant. The Cooker will be moderately hot underneath, but cool on top. In time the temperature will reach about 110° F (43° C), which is best for yoghurt. With lower temperatures it will take a little longer.

6 It may be left for 6–8 hours, or overnight. Chill before eating.

Note: A commercial starter may be bought in packets from department stores or health-food shops.

Quick method: Add an equal quantity of water to a small can of evaporated milk and bring to blood heat—when it feels just warm to the hand. Put 3 good tablespoons natural fresh yoghurt into a jug and stir until creamy. Add the warm milk, then the sweetening and flavouring (if liked). Stir well, then pour into cartons. Place on rack in Cooker and heat as described in step 5. This should set in about 3 hours.

Uses for yoghurt: A heaped tablespoon of milk powder added to 1 pint (575 ml) milk will produce a richer, firm yoghurt and this can be used as an economical substitute for cream. Plain or enriched yoghurt can be used in place of milk or cream in stews and soups and in baked cakes and breads.

BACON AND EGGS

as a frypan

Still the best of British breakfasts.

1 Remove rinds from bacon rashers and put into cold Cooker. If bacon is lean, add 2 or 3 teaspoons butter or margarine. Streaky bacon usually provides enough fat, especially if there are a number of rashers to be cooked. Turn heat to 300 (3). Fry bacon until cooked to your liking and put on a plate to keep warm.
2 Break in the eggs. If the yolks are inclined to break, put them into a cup first, then slip them carefully into Cooker. Cover with lid with vent open. Slant the Cooker a little to let more air circulate. Cook for about 2–3 minutes. Sprinkle with salt and pepper and serve with the bacon.

If mushrooms are to be cooked as well, fry them with the bacon and keep hot on the same plate. If tomatoes are to be cooked, cut in halves and fry with the eggs. Sprinkle each with a little sugar, salt and pepper.

FRENCH TOAST WITH BACON

1 Allow 6 slices from a large square loaf for 1 egg, and 4 tablespoons milk. Beat the egg, add milk and some salt and pepper and pour on to a flat plate.
2 Put required number of bacon rashers into Cooker and turn heat to 340 (4). Fry bacon until cooked and fat has run out. Lift out and keep warm on a plate. The toast will take extra fat so add about 1 tablespoon butter or margarine. Heat.
3 Dip bread quickly into egg and milk, wetting both sides without soaking too much. Fry for about 3 minutes on each side. Serve with the bacon.

Note: French toast may, of course, be served without bacon. See also Mock Pancakes (*p. 49*).

FRIED BANANAS WITH BACON AND EGGS

as a frypan

If you imagine that fried bananas for breakfast sounds more American than English, you are wrong. It was a popular idea as recently as Mrs Beeton's day and must have travelled across the Atlantic with the pioneers at an earlier date. Like so many other English dishes, it was kept alive in America but eventually died in England. Now it is home again. The eggs may be omitted and the bananas served with bacon only. For Brains, Crumbed, with Bacon see p. 128.

1 or more bananas per serving   *rashers of bacon*
egg and dry breadcrumbs or milk   *eggs*
   and flour

1 Put bacon in Cooker and heat to 340 (4). Fry until cooked and fat runs out, then keep hot on a plate.
2 Cut the bananas in halves crosswise and coat with either beaten egg and breadcrumbs, or milk and flour. Add a little butter or margarine to the pan if the bacon was not fat enough. Fry the bananas for only 2 or 3 minutes. If they are cooked for too long they will be soft.
3 The eggs could be fried at the same time. Serve the bacon with the bananas and eggs.

Fried bananas with bacon and scrambled eggs: Put bacon in Cooker and fry with heat at 340 (4). Remove and keep hot. Coat and fry the bananas as above. When cooked lift on to the plate with the bacon and keep hot. For the scrambled egg, allow 2 tablespoons milk and a little salt and pepper for each egg. Beat the eggs and add milk and seasoning. For scrambled eggs for 2 or 3 tilt the pan a little and cook at one end (*see p. 24*). For 4 or more, the whole pan may be used. Serve on buttered toast with the bacon and bananas.

SCRAMBLED EGGS

as a frypan

For 3 or 4 servings, use the Cooker level, but for smaller quantities, tilt it slightly, putting something under the legs to hold it in position.

2 teaspoons butter or margarine per egg	*salt and pepper*
	chopped parsley (optional)
1 or 2 eggs per serving	*grated cheese (optional)*
2 tablespoons milk per egg	*toast, buttered*

1 Put fat in Cooker and heat to 300 (3). Tilt if necessary, see above.
2 Beat eggs and add milk, seasoning and chopped parsley and grated cheese if used. Pour into Cooker.
3 Reduce heat to 220 (1) and cook for about 3–4 minutes. Move about with a wooden spoon as the mixture thickens. When there is still a little uncooked, lift at once on to the pieces of toast. The rest of the mixture will cook in its own heat.

Scrambled eggs with mushrooms and bacon: For each egg allow 2 oz (50 g) washed, sliced mushrooms and ½–1 rasher of streaky bacon. Cut bacon into 1 in (2·5 cm) pieces and put into hot Cooker. Add mushrooms and cook together. Pour in the egg mixture and cook as directed.

POACHED EGGS

as a poacher

1 Pour ½ pint (275 ml) water into the Cooker and heat to 220 (1). Sprinkle a teaspoon of vinegar and a teaspoon of flour over the top of the water and add a level teaspoon of salt.
2 Break in the eggs carefully (use poaching rings if you prefer).
3 Poach for 2 minutes, then begin to spoon the water over the yolk until cooked.
4 Meanwhile, make toast and spread with butter. Slip 1 egg on to each piece.

EGGS EN COCOTTE

as a bain-marie

A *cocotte* has two meanings: a 'fashionable prostitute' and a 'small straight-sided baking dish'. Here we are only interested in the latter!

butter or margarine	*1 egg per serving*
cream or milk	*salt and pepper*

1 Pour 1 pint (575 ml) water into the Cooker and turn to boiling point, about 220 (1).
2 Place the cocottes, or ramekins, in the water and put about ½ teaspoon butter into each. Allow to melt.
3 Add 1 dessertspoon cream or milk, then break 1 egg in each. Sprinkle with salt and pepper. Cover with Cooker lid and open vent. Cook in the boiling water for about 5 minutes or until white is firm but yolk still soft.

Note: If wished, a pinch of your favourite herb, or a few drops of Worcester sauce may be added.

With mushrooms: Allow about 1 dessertspoon washed, sliced mushrooms per egg and cook in the melted butter for 3 minutes before adding the eggs. Poach for 6–7 minutes.

With cheese: Add about 2 teaspoons grated cheese per egg with the butter. Add the milk or cream and the egg, then top with a little more cheese. Sprinkle with the salt and pepper and perhaps a little paprika. Poach for 5–6 minutes.

With chopped bacon: Remove rinds from streaky bacon and cut into ½ in (1·25 cm) pieces with scissors. Add to the melted butter and cook for 2 minutes before adding the milk or cream and the egg. Poach for about 5–6 minutes.

FRIED CRUMBED FISH

as a frypan   *for 3 or 4*

It has been said that 'fish should swim twice': once in the sea or river, then once in the hot fat, meaning that the fat should be deep. In fact, if you use crumbs or wheatgerm to coat the fish this is not necessary but the fat should always be deep for a batter coating.

3 or 4 fish fillets or steaks
(allow 1 or more per serving)
a little flour
2 tablespoons oil or butter,
or half and half

1 beaten egg with 1 tablespoon
water, ½ teaspoon salt and a
little pepper
coating of fine dry breadcrumbs or
wheatgerm

1 Remove any bones left in the fillets. Leave the large one in the steaks. Skin if you wish.
2 Dry the fish with kitchen paper and dust very lightly with flour.
3 Put oil or butter into Cooker and set heat at 340 (4).
4 Put beaten egg and water on to one large plate and the coating on another.
5 Dip fish first into egg, drain, and then into coating, covering well.
6 When fat is very hot, fry fish for about 3 minutes on each side. Lift on to a hot plate. Serve with lemon wedges or tartare sauce.

Fried crumbed fish with tomatoes: Before putting in the fish, remove skins from tomatoes by putting them first into boiling water, or by holding over a gas flame on a fork. Cut in halves, sprinkle with salt, pepper and a little sugar. Place in one end of the Cooker and heat through while fish is cooking.

Fried crumbed fish with pommes frites (or good old chips): Fry the chips first (*see p. 53*). Strain off the fat into a bowl through a fine strainer. Put about 2 tablespoons back into the pan, heat, and fry the fish.

STEAMED FISH

as a bain-marie

This is a gentle method of cooking fish. It remains moist, tender, and easy on the digestion. Ideal for invalids or convalescents.

1 or more fish fillets
or steaks per serving,
skinned and boned, if necessary
salt and pepper
3 tablespoons milk (for any
amount of fish)

2 teaspoons butter or margarine
1 dessertspoon homemade roux
(p. 14) or 1 dessertspoon
packet soup-mix
chopped parsley

1 Pour ¾ pint (425 ml) warm water into cold Cooker.
2 Put fish into a shallow heatproof dish. Sprinkle with salt and pepper, then pour on the milk. Add butter or margarine.
3 Place in the water, and turn to 220 (1) or boiling. Cover with either a plate or foil, then with Cooker lid. Close vent. Steam for 10–15 minutes, or until cooked. Lift out and keep warm.
4 The milk and fish liquid left could be thickened in the dish (with the water still boiling; add a little more if it has boiled off). Thicken, using either homemade roux or packet soup-mix. Pour the sauce over the fish and sprinkle with parsley.

Steamed fish with shrimps or prawns: Place shrimps or prawns in the dish with the fish and let them cook through. Arrange on top of the fish after sauce has been poured over.

Steamed fish with oyster sauce: Thaw oysters if frozen. Remove beards and add to sauce. Do not cook for more than half a minute.

Steamed fish with egg and parsley sauce: Hard-boil 1 large or 2 small eggs, then shell and chop. Add to sauce with about 1 tablespoon chopped parsley.

Steamed fish with onion sauce: At step 2 put 3 tablespoons finely chopped onions into the dish and place fish on top. When fish has cooked, lift out and use liquid to make sauce.

SPRINGTIME FISH FILLETS

This is a dish that may be cooked all the year round, but its pale green and yellow accompaniments must surely be a reminder of spring.

2–3 fish fillets, skinned and boned, and each cut in half crosswise (or less expensive cod cheeks)
2 teaspoons plain flour
1 teaspoon butter
1 tablespoon milk
1 bay leaf

salt and pepper
¼ lb (225 g) frozen peas, or fresh young peas, shelled
1 small can of sweetcorn
2 tablespoons cream
½ teaspoon sugar

1 Use a 5½–6 in (15 cm) heatproof dish. No lid needed. Rub fish with flour.
2 Pour 1 pint (575 ml) water into Cooker and heat to 300 (3).
3 Put fish into dish and add butter, milk and bay leaf. Season with salt and pepper. Put dish into the water in Cooker.
4 The peas could be cooking in a little salted water in a small dish on one side of Cooker and the sweetcorn heating in another. Put a piece of foil over all.
5 Reduce heat down to Simmer. Cover with Cooker lid and close vent.
6 Simmer for 15–20 minutes or until fish is cooked. Add more water if necessary.
7 After 10 minutes, take out peas, strain and put into a blender with cream, sugar and a little more salt and pepper. Blend to a purée, then put back into dish and heat through.
8 Pour the green pea sauce over the fish and serve with the sweetcorn.

FISH FILLETS WITH CARROT AND CAPER SAUCE

as a bain-marie

While the carrots are boiling in the Cooker, the fish is gently poaching in a shallow dish. The final creation is colourful and tasty.

1 teaspoon salt
½ lb (225 g) carrots, cleaned and sliced in rings or chopped
¾ lb (350 g) fish fillets, skinned, boned and each cut in half cross-wise

1 good teaspoon butter
salt and pepper
1 bay leaf
1 tablespoon cream or top of milk
2 teaspoons capers
chopped parsley

1 Pour 1 pint (575 ml) water into Cooker and turn heat to 220 (1). Add salt.

2 Add carrots and cover with Cooker lid. Close vent and allow to simmer for 10 minutes.

3 Place the prepared fish in a shallow dish. A 7 in (17·5 cm) freezer foil tart dish would do. Put butter on top and add the bay leaf. Sprinkle with salt and pepper.

4 Push carrots to the side and place dish in the water. Cover loosely with a piece of foil then with Cooker lid. Close vent and allow 15 minutes.

5 Take off Cooker lid, but be careful not to disturb the foil and let water fall into dish. Lift out the dish and drain fish liquid into a small saucepan. Keep fish warm.

6 Take out carrots with a slotted spoon and purée in mouli or blender until smooth.

7 Boil fish liquor until reduced to 1 tablespoon. Add carrot, cream and capers. Heat, then pour over the fish. Sprinkle with chopped parsley to give an attractive finish.

FISH FILLETS VÉRONIQUE

This well-known dish was invented by a famous French chef, Monsieur Malley of the Paris Ritz. He gave it the name of his young underchef's daughter, Véronique, who was born on the day the dish was first created. Today it is enjoyed in many parts of the world.

2 fillets of sole or other fine white fish, skinned
salt and pepper
¼ pt (150 ml) water with 4 tablespoons white wine
1 bay leaf, broken into 3 pieces

1 small onion, peeled and halved
3 oz (75 g) pitted white grapes
6 tablespoons milk or cream
1 teaspoon prepared roux (p. 14) or arrowroot
chopped parsley

1 See that there are no bones left in the fish then cut in halves lengthwise. Sprinkle with salt and pepper. Roll up, thick end to tip, and secure with small cocktail sticks.
2 Pour water and white wine into Cooker and turn to 220 (1). Put in the fish rolls, then add the bay-leaf pieces and onion halves. Put on Cooker lid and close vent. Poach for 6–8 minutes, or until fish has cooked.
3 Lift the fish rolls on to a serving-dish and keep warm.
4 Put grapes into Cooker and heat through for 1 minute. Put on to a saucer and keep warm with the fish. Remove bay leaf and onion (used for flavouring only).
5 Add milk or cream (or half and half). Thicken with 1 heaped teaspoon of your prepared roux or 1 rounded teaspoon arrowroot mixed with a little water.
6 Pour over fish and garnish with the grapes. Sprinkle with chopped parsley.

FISH WITH RICE AND EGG SAUCE

as a bain-marie

To be in the swim today, we need to save on fuel bills. In this recipe the Cooker will cope with three things at once: the fish, the rice and the hard-boiled egg.

4 oz (100 g) long-grain rice with ½ pint (275 ml) plus 3 tablespoons water
salt and pepper
1 egg
¾ lb (350 g) fish fillets, skinned (or use inexpensive cod cheeks)
2 teaspoons butter or margarine
1 tablespoon milk
1 bay leaf

SAUCE
liquid from cooking fish plus 4 tablespoons milk or cream
1 dessertspoon homemade roux (p. 14) or 1 dessertspoon packet soup-mix, pale kind
2–3 tablespoons tasty cheese, grated (optional)
2 teaspoons anchovy essence
salt and pepper
chopped parsley (optional)

1 Use 2 heatproof dishes, one for the fish about 5–5½ in (13 cm) across and one for the rice about 4 in (10 cm) across. Foil freezer dishes would do.

2 Pour 1½ pints (850 ml) water into Cooker and turn heat to 220 (1).

3 Put the rice and water with ½ teaspoon salt into smaller dish. Place in the Cooker. Put the egg in the Cooker also to hard-boil.

4 Cut fish into halves or thirds and put into larger dish. Add butter or margarine, milk, bay leaf and salt and pepper. Stand in the Cooker.

5 Cover all with a piece of foil, then with Cooker lid. Close vent. Let water boil for 15 minutes.

6 Lift out fish dish and pour the fish liquid into a small saucepan. Add milk or cream and begin to heat. Stir in the thickening (roux or soup mix) and cook until thick and smooth, stirring constantly. Stir in cheese, if used, and allow to melt. Add anchovy essence and salt and pepper to taste. Shell hard-boiled egg, chop, and add.

7 The rice should be cooked by now. Serve the fish with the sauce poured over and serve the rice separately. If wished, sprinkle with chopped parsley.

FISH CAKES

as a frypan   *makes 4–6*

These are ideal for the Cooker. The fish may be canned (salmon is excellent), fresh or smoked, or a mixture. A little smoked fish or roe gives a tang to the mixture.

½ lb (225 g) cooked or canned fish (see above)
2 oz (50 g), or 1 cup, fresh breadcrumbs
about 2–3 tablespoons liquid: use liquid from the can, or for fresh cooked fish, use milk
½ teaspoon bay-leaf powder or basil

2 teaspoons anchovy essence
salt and pepper
2 tablespoons fat or 3 tablespoons oil
1 egg, beaten
fine dry breadcrumbs, crushed cornflakes or wheatgerm, for coating

1   Mash fish in a bowl and add breadcrumbs, liquid, herb, anchovy essence and seasoning. Mix well.
2   Put fat or oil into Cooker, turn to 340 (4) and leave to heat.
3   Add beaten egg to mixture. Form into cakes about ¾ in (2 cm) thick and 2½–3 in (7 cm) across. Press into coating, covering both sides.
4   When light goes out and fat is very hot, fry cakes for about 4 minutes on each side.

Note: The breadcrumbs can be replaced with either 8 oz (225 g) cooked rice or 6 oz (175 g) mashed potatoes.

Salmon fish cakes: Add 1 teaspoon tomato purée and ½ teaspoon sugar when mashing the canned salmon.

LAYERED RED AND GREEN FISH SAVOURY

as a bain-marie   *serves 4*

New, colourful and deliciously flavoured, this dish could extend the
repertoire of those who are on meatless diets or whose appetites
need pepping up.

3 heaped tablespoons dry
  breadcrumbs
1 lb (½ kg) cod, or other fish,
  fillets, skinned (or use
  inexpensive cod cheeks)
1 level tablespoon plain flour
½ lb (¼ kg) cucumber, peeled and
  sliced

salt and pepper
½ lb (225 g) tomatoes, skinned and
  sliced
sugar
basil
2 tablespoons single cream,
  evaporated milk or yoghurt
chopped parsley

1 Use a 6–6½ in (16 cm) straight-sided heatproof dish about 2 in
  (5 cm) deep. A soufflé dish is ideal. Put 2 tablespoons of the
  breadcrumbs on the bottom. Spread evenly.
2 Cut fish into 2 in (5 cm) pieces (cod cheeks will need a little
  trimming). Toss in the flour.
3 Pour 1½ pints (850 ml) water into Cooker and set heat at 220 (1).
4 Put half the fish into dish, then half the prepared cucumber.
  Sprinkle with salt and pepper.
5 Cover with half the prepared tomatoes and sprinkle with a little
  sugar and basil.
6 Repeat with fish, seasoning, cucumber, tomatoes, sugar and basil.
  Sprinkle with the third tablespoon of breadcrumbs. Pour in the
  cream, evaporated milk or yoghurt.
7 Place dish in the boiling water. Cover loosely with a piece of foil
  to prevent steam getting in. Cover with Cooker lid and close vent.
  Allow about 30–35 minutes. Let the water boil very gently, but do
  not allow it to go off the boil.
8 When cooked, sprinkle with parsley.

PLAICE SOUFFLÉ AND FRIEND

as a bain-marie   *serves 4*

The 'friend' of the plaice could be anything tasty such as canned crab, tuna fish, salmon, smoked roe or finnan haddock. Think of the recipe for a luncheon or supper dish or the first course of an elegant meal.

about ¾ lb (350 g) plaice, skinned
    and boned
2–4 oz (50–100 g) of one of the
    'friends' suggested above
3 tablespoons white wine or milk

1 bay leaf
salt and pepper
3 teaspoons anchovy essence
1 tablespoon chopped parsley
2 eggs

1 Poach the plaice as suggested on p. 29, using the 3 tablespoons wine or milk and the bay leaf and seasoning.
2 Strain off the liquid and make up to ½ pint (275 ml) with milk or cream. Make Cream Sauce (*p. 189*) with this. Let it cool a little.
3 Use a 6–6½ in (16 cm) soufflé dish and grease well.
4 Pour 2 pints (1¼ litres) water into Cooker and set heat at 220 (1). Put in rack.
5 Mash or blend the fish and 'friend' with anchovy essence. Stir into sauce. Add parsley.
6 Separate the eggs, dropping the whites into a bowl. Beat the yolks and stir into the fish mixture. Taste and add salt and pepper.
7 Beat the egg whites until very stiff and fold into the mixture. Use only a few strokes and do not beat. Tip into soufflé dish and place on rack. Cover with Cooker lid and open vent. Let the water boil gently and allow 1 hour 5 minutes. Try not to look during cooking time. Serve at once.

Additions: Colourful or piquant 'acquaintances' may be added, such as green peas, chopped gherkins, capers, finely slithered almonds or sweetcorn kernels.

FISH, SPINACH AND BEANS
ALL-IN-TOGETHER

as a bain-marie

You will need three dishes that will fit comfortably into the Cooker:
two small ones for the spinach and beans and one larger size for the
fish. Freezer foil containers may be used.

3 teaspoons butter or margarine
½–¾ lb (225–350 g) fish fillets,
    skinned
salt and pepper
1 bay leaf
½ lb (225 g) packet of frozen
    spinach (or any other
    vegetable, for example peas)

1 small can of beans such as
    haricots (white or green), butter
    beans or lima beans
1 standard egg
4 tablespoons milk

1 For dishes, see above. Thaw spinach.
2 Smear 1 teaspoon butter or margarine over the bottom of the fish
   dish and put in the fish. Sprinkle with salt and pepper and add bay
   leaf.
3 Pour 1 pint (575 ml) water into Cooker and turn heat to 220 (1).
4 Put 1 teaspoon butter, 3 tablespoons boiling water and a little
   salt into one of the smaller dishes and add spinach (or other
   vegetable). Put into Cooker. Cover with foil or a small saucer.
5 Drain salty liquid from beans and put the drained beans into the
   other small dish. Add 1 teaspoon butter and cover with foil or a
   small saucer. Put into Cooker.
6 Beat the egg with the milk and pour over fish. Put into Cooker
   and cover with foil.
7 Cover with Cooker lid and close vent. Let water boil and allow 15
   minutes.

Fish, spinach and sweetcorn: Use a small can of sweetcorn
kernels instead of the beans.

FISH PIE WITH CHEESE SAUCE

An excellent choice when friends come to lunch. The potato, the fish-and-onion mixture and the cheese sauce could all be cooked the day before, leaving only the assembly for the morning. Don't apologize for using dried potato: peeling the brutes is not the most joyous of pastimes.

1 tablespoon butter
1 lb (½ kg) fresh potatoes, cooked and mashed, or 3 oz (75 g) dried potato mixed with about ½ pint (275 ml) boiling milk and water
1 onion, peeled and chopped
1 bay leaf

1 lb (½ kg) white fish, skinned and boned
salt and pepper
milk
chopped parsley
2 hard-boiled eggs
cheese sauce (p. 189)

1   Use a deep 6½–7 in (17 cm) heatproof dish.
2   Add butter to the prepared mashed potato.
3   Put onions and 4 tablespoons water into a saucepan. Add bay leaf. Cover with lid and simmer for 5 minutes.
4   Cut fish into 2 in (5 cm) pieces and add. Season with salt and pepper. Cover again and simmer for another 5 minutes. Remove from heat.
5   Pour liquid into a measuring jug and make up to ½ pint (275 ml) with milk.
6   Put fish and onions into dish and sprinkle generously with chopped parsley.
7   Put rack in Cooker and turn heat to 420 (6).
8   Shell hard-boiled eggs and cut into quarters. Add to fish. Pour the cheese sauce over.
9   Spread with the potato and neaten with fork lines, or pipe on the potato using a potato rose. Place dish on rack and cover with Cooker lid. Open vent. Allow 20 minutes.

FISH RISOTTO

as a cook-and-serve dish   *serves 4–6*

A risotto is a dish based on rice, to which many additions can be
made. For instance, ingredients such as tomatoes, olives, lobster,
crabmeat, prawns, cheese and various vegetables could either
replace or be added to those suggested below.

2 teaspoons oil or butter
2 rashers of streaky bacon, rinds
  removed
1 large onion, peeled and
  chopped, or use frozen chopped
  onions
2 sticks of celery, chopped
8–10 oz (225–275 g) long-grain
  rice (see Note)
about 12 oz (350 g) fish, skinned
  and boned (a proportion could
  be smoked)

1¼–1½ pints (725–850 ml) warm
  water (depending on amount of
  rice)
1 chicken stock cube
2 bay leaves
garlic (optional)
salt and pepper
4 oz (100 g) mushrooms, washed
  and sliced (see above for other
  possible additions)

1 Put oil or butter into Cooker and turn to 300 (3).
2 Cut bacon into 1 in (2·5 cm) pieces and fry until sizzling.
3 Add onion and continue frying for 3 minutes. Add celery.
4 Stir in rice and cook for 2 minutes, then add fish, cut into 2 in
   (50 cm) pieces.
5 Add water, crumbled stock cube, bay leaves and garlic, if liked.
   Stir together. Season with salt and pepper.
6 Cover with Cooker lid and close vent. Cook gently for about 15–18
   minutes. Add more water if necessary.
7 Add the mushrooms about 6 minutes before rice is cooked or, if
   preferred, fry them first in a little butter and use as a garnish.
   To add colour, frozen or canned mixed vegetables may be added
   about 6 minutes before cooking is completed.

Note: Wholegrain rice will take much longer to cook, so at step 4 add
the water after rice has been fried, turn to Simmer, cover with
Cooker lid and close vent, and cook it for 30 minutes before adding
the fish; and, because of the longer cooking time needed, add more
water. Other varieties of brown rice take less time; discovering which
is which is a question of following the directions if it comes in a
packet, or of learning by experience.

PARTY PAELLA

A paella is a glorified Fish Risotto (*p. 37*): all we need to do is to add to it some or all of the other traditional ingredients. The Spanish word *paella* refers not to the food, but to the dish in which it is cooked. In size and shape it is similar to the Cooker, so the recipe is particularly appropriate.

Fish Risotto (p. 37)
¼ cooked chicken or 2 cooked
   chicken breasts
4 oz (100 g) garlic sausage
6 oz (175 g) cooked large prawns
¼ lb (225 g) ripe tomatoes

2 tablespoons oil or butter
salt and pepper
¼ teaspoon saffron
16 mussels (optional) (see Note)
parsley

1 Make the fish risotto and while it is cooking prepare the additional ingredients.
2 Cut cooked chicken into pieces. Slice the sausage and thaw the prawns if frozen. Skin the tomatoes, by first either putting them into boiling water or holding them over a gas flame on a fork, then remove skins. Keep warm.
3 In another pan, heat the oil or butter and add the chicken, sausage and prawns. Sprinkle with salt and pepper and fry for 3 minutes.
4 Add saffron to cooked fish risotto then arrange the additional ingredients on top, including the mussels if used. With 'studied carelessness', pop the tomato slices here and there to add colour, and garnish with sprigs of parsley.
5 Reduce Cooker heat to below Simmer. The food should keep hot, but not cook any more.

Note: A true Spanish paella should include mussels in their shells but it is often made without. Scrub and rinse the mussels well and examine them carefully. If they are not tight shut (or do not shut at a sharp tap) discard them. Put the rest into a large bowl or saucepan of boiling water, removing them as the shells open. All should have opened within about 5 minutes; some might take a little longer. Arrange on top of the paella.

STUFFED FISH ROLLS

as a frypan   *makes 4*

Many different types of fish come from many different oceans, rivers and lakes and some whose names are familiar to one country are strange to others. But most fish, however exotic, may be filleted, and it is fillets that you will need for this recipe.

2 slender fillets of fish
3 oz (75 g) smoked roe or substitute (see below)
3 rounded tablespoons fresh breadcrumbs
1 tablespoon cream, evaporated milk or top of the milk, or enough to make a damp paste

3 tablespoons corn oil or other cooking oil
1 egg
1 tablespoon water
salt and pepper
fine dry breadcrumbs
skinned tomatoes and washed, sliced mushrooms as accompaniments (optional)

1 Buy fillets skinned. Cut in halves lengthwise. If the fish is cod, use about 7 in (17·5 cm) of the thin end.

2 Combine the roe, fresh breadcrumbs and binding liquid.

3 Pour oil into Cooker and turn heat to 380 (5).

4 Spread stuffing on to the long slender pieces of fish and roll up. Secure with cocktail sticks.

5 Beat the egg on a plate with the water and seasoning. Put dry breadcrumbs on to another plate.

6 Brush rolls with the egg, then roll in breadcrumbs, to cover completely.

7 When Cooker light has gone out, spread the oil evenly and fry the rolls, turning as they brown. When browned, reduce heat to 300 (3) and let them cook through—about 10–15 minutes. Tomatoes and mushrooms could be frying at the same time.

STUFFING VARIATIONS

Instead of the smoked roe, use mashed sardines and add 1 teaspoon Worcester sauce, or use mashed shrimps or prawns and anchovy essence instead of the cream or milk.

GERI'S MULTI COOKER OMELETTE

as an omelette pan   *serves 2*

Because of the shape of the Multi Cooker, this omelette will be rectangular but its quality is not diminished because of that. Bacon may be cooked at the same time.

2 teaspoons butter
rashers of bacon, rinds removed,
    either left whole or cut into
    pieces
mushrooms, washed and sliced
    (optional)

2 eggs
2 tablespoons water
2 tablespoons milk
salt and pepper

1 Put butter into Cooker and turn heat to 340 (4). When melted brush it over the base of the Cooker. Lower heat to 300 (3).
2 Tilt the Cooker by placing a thin piece of wood or cardboard under the back legs. Put bacon on the higher side and leave it to cook gently. Mushrooms may be cooked at the same time as the bacon.
3 Put the eggs, liquid and seasoning into a bowl. Beat for about $\frac{1}{4}$ minute only.
4 Have a fish slice in the right hand and the bowl in the left. Pour the mixture into the near end of the Cooker and as it cooks use the fish slice to form it into a rectangle. Loosen the mixture from outer edges. Cook until the top is still not quite set, then divide the rectangle in two and fold each half. The omelette should be lightly browned. Serve at once with the bacon.

Cheese omelette: Add about 2 tablespoons grated Cheddar or Parmesan to the egg mixture after beating, or sprinkle it on the omelette just before folding over.

BRUNCH OMELETTE (sort-of)

as an omelette pan   *serves 4*

Not quite breakfast, not quite lunch. Not quite an omellete, not quite scrambled egg. Thick, smooth and delicious, and combining three favourite things: eggs, bacon and cheese. Variations below.

3 or 4 rashers of streaky bacon, rinds removed and cut into 1¼ in (3·75 cm) pieces
5 eggs, preferably large
¼ pint (150 ml) milk

5 tablespoons water
4 oz (100 g) Parmesan or Cheddar cheese, grated
salt and pepper
seasoning salt

1 Drop the pieces of bacon into the Cooker and turn heat to 300 (3).
2 Beat the eggs and add milk, water, cheese and seasoning.
3 When bacon is sizzling and fat has run out, pour in the egg mixture and at once turn heat down to 220 (1) to set the eggs. Cover with Cooker lid and open vent.
4 Leave undisturbed until set, about 8–10 minutes.
5 To serve, cut into rectangular pieces and lift out with a palette-knife, turning over to show the browned underside.

With tomatoes: Replace the water with 3 medium-sized skinned tomatoes. Add 1 or 2 teaspoons Worcester sauce and 1 teaspoon sugar.

With mushrooms: Fry 6 oz (175 g) washed, sliced mushrooms with the bacon.

Spanish omelette: Slice left-over potatoes and fry with the bacon and finely sliced onions. Pour the mixture on top.

With cooked prawns or shrimps: After pouring in the mixture sprinkle in about 4 oz (100 g) prawns or shrimps.

With olives or gherkins: After pouring in the mixture add sliced stuffed olives or sliced gherkins in any quantity.

AWAY-DAY BEAN CASSEROLE

A bean casserole needs slow cooking. This one may be put into the Cooker before leaving for work and left to cook until supper time. In flavour it is similar to Boston Baked Beans.

8 oz (225 g) haricot beans or butter beans
1 pint (575 ml) hot water
½ pint (275 ml) canned peeled tomatoes with juice
2 tablespoons golden syrup
1 onion, peeled and finely chopped
¼ lb (100 g) bacon, or more if liked, cut into pieces

1 chicken stock cube
1 teaspoon basil
2 teaspoons French mustard
1–2 teaspoons Worcester sauce
salt and pepper (or replace some of the salt with 2 teaspoons soy sauce)
grated cheese

1 Because of the long cooking, the beans need not be soaked. Rinse them and tip into a casserole dish. Add the water.
2 Put rack in Cooker and turn heat to 420 (6).
3 Add the tomatoes, syrup, onion, bacon, crumbled stock cube, basil, mustard and Worcester sauce to beans in casserole.
4 Place casserole on rack and when liquid begins to bubble, stir, then turn down to Simmer. Cover with casserole lid and Cooker lid and close vent.
5 Allow 9 hours.
6 Before serving, season with salt and pepper and top generously with grated cheese.

Additions: Other ingredients could include sausages, mushrooms, garlic, slices of chicken, finely cut celery and carrots.

FRIED BUCKWHEAT CAKES

These may replace potatoes with grills or other meats, or with vegetables and a sauce, such as Cheese or Mushroom Sauce (*p. 189*), for a vegetarian meal.

2 oz (50 g) toasted buckwheat
½ pint (275 ml) water
¼ teaspoon salt and a little pepper
¼ teaspoon sage

1 egg yolk; for double the quantity
   use the whole egg
oil or fat for frying

1 Put buckwheat, water and seasoning into a saucepan and boil for about 5–8 minutes, until very thick. Add sage.
2 Tip into a bowl and allow to cool.
3 Beat egg yolk and stir in. Taste and add more seasoning if necessary.
4 If chops, sausages or other meats are frying, add only a small amount of extra fat. If not, put 2 tablespoons oil or other fat in Cooker and heat to 380 (5). Allow fat to get hot.
5 With floury hands form the buckwheat into flat cakes about ½–¾ in (1·5 cm) thick and fry on both sides until browned. (If frying chops or sausages at the same time start cooking the buckwheat cakes about 10 minutes before the meat is ready.)

Buckwheat cakes with cheese topping: After frying the buckwheat cakes, heat grill, then top each cake with a generous quantity of grated tasty cheese. Sprinkle with salt and pepper, and grill. After cheese has melted and sizzled, dust with paprika.

Buckwheat cakes and bacon for breakfast: Cook the buckwheat the day before and form into cakes either after cooking or in the morning. Cook the bacon first and keep hot, then fry the buckwheat cakes in the bacon fat, adding fat or oil if the bacon is lean.

CHEESE FONDUE

If you have an electric plug near the table or a suitable extension lead, the Multi Cooker is the perfect vessel to keep your fondue constantly at the right temperature. Ideal for a fondue party.

1 clove of garlic
1 lb (½ kg) Swiss cheese, or English processed slices
¼ pint (150 ml) milk
1 rounded teaspoon cornflour

1 teaspoon mustard
¼ pint (150 ml) white wine or cider
salt and pepper
1 teaspoon sugar

1 Use a deep pottery or heavy iron-and-enamel dish and put into Cooker. Set heat at 340 (4) or medium heat. Rub inside of dish with a cut clove of garlic.
2 Cut cheese into small pieces and add to dish. Let it begin to melt.
3 Put milk into a small saucepan and heat. Mix cornflour and mustard with 2 tablespoons cold water until smooth and stir in. Cook and stir until thick. Remove from heat and stir in the wine or cider. Season with a little salt and pepper. Add sugar.
4 Add to cheese and stir until cheese has completely melted.
5 Reduce heat to a low simmering point. The Cooker should cool so that it is fairly hot, but not so hot it can't be touched. The fondue should be thick. If it is not, your guests will find it difficult not to drip it on to your table or carpet! But if it is too thick, add more wine.

Provide some or all of the following:

French bread, toasted and cut into 1½ in (3·75 cm) pieces. Impale on forks or skewers.

Long bread sticks.

Rye bread, toasted and cut into 1½ in (3·75 cm) squares. Impale on forks or skewers.

Crispbread, snapped lengthwise.

CHEESE, HAM AND RICE CUSTARD

as a bain-marie

If you keep cooked rice in the deep freeze or have some left over from another meal, this would be a quick, tasty way to use it.

2–3 oz (50–75 g) chopped ham
3 oz (75 g), or more, tasty cheese, grated
2 eggs
½ pint (275 ml) milk, heated

6 oz (175 g), or 6 rounded tablespoons, cooked rice
salt and pepper
2 oz (50 g) mushrooms, washed and sliced (optional)

1 Use a 5½–6 in (14·5 cm) soufflé dish or pie dish.
2 Place the ham and cheese in the dish.
3 Pour 1½ pints (850 ml) water into Cooker and turn heat to 220 (1).
4 Beat the eggs in a bowl. Heat the milk and add. Add the rice and seasoning, and mushrooms if liked. Tip into dish and place in the water.
5 Cover with a plate, then with Cooker lid. Close vent. Cook for 30 minutes, allowing the water to bubble.

Note: Peas, beans or another suitable vegetable could be cooked at the same time in a second container. A small, deep, foil freezer dish would do. If it hasn't a lid, cover with a saucer or a piece of foil.

Cheese, ham and sweetcorn custard: Add canned sweetcorn kernels instead of the rice.

Cheese, fish and rice custard: Add 4–6 oz (125–175 g) flaked cooked fish instead of the ham.

For added piquancy: If you like a more piquant flavour, add 1 or 2 teaspoons tomato purée, 2 teaspoons capers, or 1 or 2 teaspoons Worcester sauce. 2 or 3 teaspoons anchovy essence could be added if using fish variation above.

Scalloped Savoury Dishes

This title covers a multitude of luncheon or supper dishes, all made similarly but with different ingredients. 'Scalloped' is the name given to dishes which have a topping of buttered breadcrumbs.

SCALLOPED EGG AND HAM SAVOURY WITH BUCKWHEAT

as an oven   *serves 2*

2 oz (50 g), or more, chopped bacon or ham
1 oz (25 g) toasted buckwheat
¼ pint (150 ml) water
salt and pepper
2 hard-boiled eggs

sauce made with ¼ pint (150 ml) milk and 1 level tablespoon packet soup-mix
topping of 3 heaped tablespoons dry breadcrumbs and 1 tablespoon grated cheese

1 If bacon is to be used, cut it into 1 in (2·5 cm) pieces and fry in the saucepan you will use to cook the buckwheat.
2 Lift it out, then add buckwheat, water and salt and pepper. Cook for about 8–10 minutes, covered with lid.
3 Put rack in Cooker and turn to 420 (6).
4 Use a 5–5½ in (13 cm) soufflé dish, pie dish or freezer foil dish. Put in the cooked buckwheat.
5 Shell and chop the eggs and arrange on top of the buckwheat, then add the bacon or ham. Pour sauce over then spread with the topping.
6 Place dish on rack and cover with Cooker lid. Open vent. Allow about 20 minutes.

Fish, egg and sweetcorn savoury: Use a small can of cream-style sweetcorn instead of the buckwheat, and flaked cooked fish instead of the bacon or ham.

Asparagus and egg savoury: Cover buckwheat (or sweetcorn) with quartered hard-boiled eggs and asparagus tips. Use part asparagus liquid for the sauce.

VEGETARIAN LENTIL RISSOLES

There sometimes seems to be confusion between lentils and split peas. Lentils are tiny and a bright pinky-red. Split peas are larger, a pale yellow-pink, or green, and take twice as long to cook. Green lentils are also available.

6 oz (175 g) or 6 rounded tablespoons red lentils
1 onion, peeled and chopped
½ pint (275 ml) water
a few bacon rinds or a rasher of bacon (optional)
1 small teaspoon sage
2 teaspoons tomato purée
salt and pepper

3–4 oz (75–100 g) Parmesan or Cheddar cheese, grated
1 egg, beaten
2 tablespoons oil, lard or other cooking fat
fine dry breadcrumbs or wheatgerm
tomatoes (optional)

1 Put into a saucepan (or pressure cooker, *see Note*) the lentils, onions, water, bacon (if liked), sage, tomato purée and seasoning. Cover with lid and simmer gently, stirring frequently, for about 45–60 minutes. It will become a thick smooth paste. Remove rasher or rinds.
2 Add cheese and egg, then pour on to a plate and allow to cool.
3 Put fat into Cooker and heat to 340 (4).
4 Form mixture into flat cakes about ¾ in (2 cm) thick and 2½–3 in (7 cm) across. Coat with breadcrumbs or wheatgerm and fry for 4–5 minutes on each side. Tomatoes, skinned and halved, may be fried at the same time. Sprinkle them with a little salt, pepper and sugar.

Note: The preliminary cooking of the lentils may be done in a pressure cooker. Put lentils and other ingredients into a bowl but reduce water to 7½ fl oz (225 ml). Cover tightly with foil. Put into pressure cooker with 1 pint (575 ml) water and allow 15 minutes at 15 lb or high pressure.

STUFFED PANCAKES, SAVOURY

as a frypan or as a griddle pan   *makes about 10*

Make the pancake mixture as described on p. 48. If the pancakes are to be served later, place one on top of the other with thin wrapping between. They may be reheated after they have been filled and rolled.

FILLINGS

Chicken and ham: Chop finely (or use mincer or blender) ¾ lb (350 g) cooked chicken and ¼ lb (100 g) cooked ham. Season with salt and pepper and add something piquant such as capers, chopped gherkins or chopped olives. Moisten with ¼ pint (150 ml) Cream Sauce (*p. 189*), cream, yoghurt or evaporated milk. Put 2 tablespoons of the mixture in the centre of each pancake and roll up. They may be served at once, or laid side by side in a heatproof dish and heated through in the Cooker.

Bacon, onion and mushrooms: Cut 3 oz (75 g) streaky bacon into 1 in (2·5 cm) pieces and begin to fry for 5 minutes in Cooker or smaller frying pan with 1 finely chopped onion. Add 4 oz (100 g) washed, sliced mushrooms and fry for 2 minutes. Add 6 tablespoons fresh breadcrumbs and ½ teaspoon thyme.

Scrambled egg with cheese and chopped olives or gherkins: Scramble 3 eggs as described on p. 24 and add 4 oz (100 g) grated tasty cheese and 2 tablespoons chopped olives or gherkins. Season well with salt, or celery salt, and pepper and, if desired, ½ teaspoon powdered bay leaf.

Asparagus and cheese: Mash 4 oz (100 g) cream cheese with 4 tablespoons cream or evaporated milk and season with salt and pepper. Spread this on to the pancakes and arrange 2 asparagus spears on each. Roll up.

Seafood: Stir 4 oz (100 g) chopped cooked prawns and 4 oz (100 g) crabmeat or tuna fish into Cream Sauce (*p. 189*) and flavour with anchovy essence to taste.

PEGGY'S LUSCIOUS CHEESE PANCAKES

as a frypan or as a griddle pan   *makes 6 large pancakes*

'Fattening,' says Peggy, 'but oh, so more-ish!' True. The mixture makes a thicker pancake than the traditional one and it is served without rolling. I would say it is nourishing rather than fattening. It is full of good protein and very little starch.

3 large eggs, separated
8 oz (225 g) cottage cheese
3 oz (75 g) plain flour

2 tablespoons salad oil
salt and pepper

1 Beat the egg whites until stiff.
2 Without washing the beater, beat together in another bowl the egg yolks, cheese, flour, oil and seasoning.
3 Stir in the egg whites, but do not beat. Pour mixture into a jug.
4 Brush Cooker generously with oil or butter and turn heat to 340 (4).
5 When light goes out, pour mixture from about 6 in (15 cm) above the Cooker until it spreads to a 6 in (15 cm) pancake.
6 Cook until bubbles appear on the surface, then flip over and cook on the other side until golden. Brush Cooker again with a little more oil or butter and repeat until mixture is used up.
7 Preferably eat warm, but these pancakes are also good cold when fresh.

MOCK PANCAKES

These are simple and delicious.

See recipe for French Toast on p. 22. Cut the bread thinly, preferably from a large square loaf. Dip into the egg and milk and fry as directed in the recipe. They may be used in the same way as real pancakes, served either rolled or flat, and it is difficult to tell the difference, especially when rolled.

FRITTERS, SAVOURY

as a frypan

Fritter batter: Beat 1 large egg in a bowl with 1 tablespoon milk. Sieve in 4 oz (100 g) plain flour and add ½ teaspoon salt. Thin with 6 tablespooons milk.

To be cooked to a crisp golden finish, fritters need about ½ in (1·25 cm) very hot oil or other fat. In the Multicooker, ¾ pint (425 ml) vegetable or corn oil is sufficient. Have fritter batter ready, then pour oil into Multi Cooker. Turn heat to 420 (6) and heat for about 8–10 minutes. To test, drop a small teaspoon of the batter into the oil. If it sizzles with excitement and turns golden in 10 seconds it is ready. The oil should reach 375° F (188° C).

Sweetcorn fritters: Use sweetcorn kernels, either canned or frozen. Make fritter batter and stir in the well-drained kernels. Add 1 teaspoon sugar. When fat is at correct temperature, drop mixture from the end of a tablespoon into the hot fat and fry for about 2–3 minutes on each side. Drain on kitchen paper. The quantity of fritter batter given above and an 11 oz (300 g) can will make 17 fritters.

Oyster fritters: Beard the oysters and dip each separately into the batter. When fat is at correct temperature fry oysters for about 2 minutes on each side. Drain on kitchen paper. For a dozen oysters, use half the amount of batter given above.

Aubergine fritters with bacon: This is a good breakfast dish. Slice the aubergine into ¼ in (0·5 cm) slices. Do not peel. Drop into a bowl of salted cold water and leave for 20 minutes or longer. Fry bacon in Cooker and lift out. Keep hot. Drain aubergine slices and rinse with water. Dab dry with kitchen paper. Add 3 tablespoons oil to pan and when very hot, dip slices in the batter and fry for about 2 minutes on each side. Drain on kitchen paper. The quantity of fritter batter above will be sufficient for about two medium aubergines.

TOASTED SANDWICHES

as a toaster

The Cooker will crisp and brown the sandwiches in only about $1\frac{1}{2}$–2 minutes on either side which when compared with the grill means a great saving of time and fuel.

1. Make your chosen sandwich filling or fillings (*see below*) and make sandwiches in the usual way.
2. Heat Cooker to 300 (3).
3. Spread the top of each sandwich with softened butter, then put into Cooker with buttered side down. Toast until browned, then spread tops with butter and turn over. If toasting too slowly, raise the heat.
4. Serve with lettuce and salad vegetables, and add pickles if liked.

FILLINGS

Egg and cheese foundation mixture: In a small saucepan beat 1 or more eggs. For each egg add 2 tablespoons milk and 2 oz (50 g) grated, tasty cheese. Season with salt and pepper and add a little seasoning salt, mustard or other piquant flavouring. Cook and stir until scrambled. Remove from heat when just set. Such additions as chopped ham or chicken, chopped gherkins, olives or capers may then be added to this foundation.

Egg and cheese with bacon: Follow recipe for foundation mixture, above, but first fry the bacon, allowing $\frac{1}{2}$ rasher for each egg. Cut into $\frac{1}{2}$ in (1·25 cm) pieces and fry until just crisp, then add the beaten egg, the milk and the cheese.

Chopped hard-boiled eggs with walnuts: Add finely chopped walnuts to chopped hard-boiled eggs (there should be about twice as much egg as walnut) and moisten with a little cream, mayonnaise or yoghurt. Season with salt and pepper and perhaps a little seasoning salt.

Liver pâté with slices of egg or tomato: Spread buttered bread with pâté and cover with slices of hard-boiled egg or tomato, or both.

RATATOUILLE

A combination of vegetables with an exotic flavour and attractive appearance. It may be served as a starter, as an accompaniment to sautéd or grilled meats, fish or vegetarian dishes, or as a main dish sprinkled generously with cheese.

1 aubergine, about 8 oz (225 g)
½ lb (225 g) courgettes
1 tablespoon oil or butter
1 large Spanish onion, peeled
* and sliced*
1 green pepper, about 4 oz (100 g)
1 or 2 cloves of garlic, well
* crushed*

1 teaspoon basil (optional)
½ lb (225 g) tomatoes, peeled
* and sliced (or a 14 oz (390 g)*
* tin*
2 teaspoons honey (optional)
salt and pepper

1. Slice, but do not peel, the aubergine and drop into a bowl of cold salted water.
2. Cut courgettes lengthwise and remove seeds. Cut into 1 in (2· cm) pieces.
3. Put oil or butter into Cooker and turn heat to 340 (4). Add onion
4. Lift aubergine slices from water and rinse through a strainer to remove salt and bitter juices. Drain well, add to pan and fry with the onion for 5 minutes, adding garlic.
5. Stir in courgettes, and basil if used. Cover with Cooker lid and close vent. Cook for another 10 minutes.
6. Meanwhile, remove seeds and membrane from green pepper and cut into rough slices. Add to Cooker with the tomatoes, honey and seasoning. Cover again with Cooker lid and close vent. Allow another 5 minutes. The short time of 5 minutes will not spoil the colour of the green peppers and tomatoes.

Mock ratatouille: This may be made with a number of different vegetables, using a base of tomatoes and onion. Use peeled, sliced cucumber instead of the aubergine, with any other vegetables you wish.

POMMES FRITES OR CHIPS

as a fryer

For deep or semi-deep frying in the home kitchen, oil has advantages over lard and other cooking fats. Provided it is clear with no little bits of solids floating in it, it will reach the right temperature without splashing and without steaming up the kitchen with misty smoke. I was once a devotee of lard, but now I prefer oil, especially corn oil, soya bean oil or nut oil.

To save time buy the frozen (but not pre-fried) prepared potato chips. Chips may be cut and prepared at home but they take longer to do. The Note below gives the method.

1 lb (½ kg) potatoes, either prepared frozen or fresh, cut into fingers (see Note)

1 pint (½ litre) vegetable oil or corn oil
salt and pepper

1 Thaw the frozen chips. Dry with kitchen paper if wet.
2 Pour oil into Cooker and turn heat to 420 (6). If you have a thermometer, bring temperature of oil to 375° F (190° C). If not, let oil heat for about 8 minutes then test. Put a small cube of stale bread into the oil and if it turns a golden brown on both sides in 10 seconds, the oil is ready.
3 Slip in the chips about ½ lb (225 g) at a time. Fry, moving the chips about with a spatula, for about 5–6 minutes, or until they are as golden as you wish.
4 Lift out with a slotted spoon, drain on kitchen paper and keep hot. Sprinkle with salt and pepper. Repeat with the remaining chips.

Note: To make your own chips from raw potatoes—cut potatoes into fingers and drop into cold water. Soak for about 10 minutes, then dry well. To get the best results, fry the chips for 1 minute in the hot oil, then lift out with a slotted spoon. Heat the oil again for 3 minutes to bring it back to the right temperature, then fry the chips until golden and crisp.

STUFFED BAKED POTATOES

as an oven

The potatoes should be baked either on the rack or on a folded piece of foil on the floor of the Cooker. They are better if they are not wrapped in foil. A few of the possible fillings are listed below.

whole large old potatoes, not waxy types; Whites are excellent for baking

butter
Filling (see below)
dry breadcrumbs

1 Put rack or a folded piece of foil into Cooker and heat to 420 (6).
2 Scrub the potatoes well. Some people like to brush them with oil, but I prefer them as they are.
3 Place potatoes on rack or foil. Cover with Cooker lid and open vent. Allow $1\frac{1}{4}$–$1\frac{1}{2}$ hours, or longer if still not cooked.
4 Lift out and cut each in half lengthwise. Scoop out potato into a bowl, leaving a $\frac{1}{4}$ in (0·5 cm) shell.
5 To the scooped-out potato add 1 teaspoon butter for each half. Add filling and mix well with the potato. Pile into potato shells and sprinkle with fine dry breadcrumbs. Put back into Cooker to reheat. Serve on lettuce leaves and with a salad.

FILLINGS

Grated cheese with chopped chives: Allow 1 tablespoon grated Parmesan or Cheddar cheese for each half and lots of chopped chives. Season with salt and pepper. Other additions could include seasoning salt, herb-and-spice salt, curry powder, Worcester sauce or anchovy essence.

Chopped fried bacon or chopped ham with cheese: Allow 1 oz (25 g) chopped fried bacon or finely chopped ham and $\frac{1}{2}$ oz (13 g) grated cheese for each half potato. Season well.

Chopped hard-boiled eggs with cheese and ham: For 2 potatoes allow 1 chopped hard boiled egg, 1 oz (25 g) grated cheese and 2 oz (50 g) chopped ham. Season well.

SCALLOPED POTATOES, NEW WAY?

One makes claims with caution: 'There is no new thing under the sun', says the Bible; so perhaps someone has already thought of this recipe?

1 rounded tablespoon butter
1 teaspoon mint jelly or finely chopped fresh mint
1 scant teaspoon dried tarragon
1 lb (½ kg) potatoes
¼ pint (150 ml) milk plus 4 tablespoons milk

1 level tablespoon packet soup-mix, pale type, such as celery, leek, etc.
1 level teaspoon salt and a little pepper
topping of 4 heaped tablespoons breadcrumbs, wheatgerm or crushed cornflakes

1 Use a heatproof dish about 5½–6 in (14·5 cm) across and 2½–3 in (6 cm) deep. Add butter and put into Cooker. Turn heat to 420 (6) and let butter melt. Add mint and tarragon.

2 Peel and finely slice the potatoes and add. Stir until they are coated with butter and herbs.

3 Heat milk in a small saucepan. Mix the soup mix with 1 tablespoon water and stir in. Cook, stirring, until smooth and add seasoning. Pour over the potatoes.

4 Cover loosely with a piece of foil then with Cooker lid. Close vent. Leave at the high heat for 15 minutes, then turn down to 300 (3).

5 After 1 hour remove lid and foil and cover with chosen topping. Cover again with lid and open vent. Allow another 30 minutes or until potatoes are soft.

Note: If the Cooker is being used for a casserole which takes about 1½–1¾ hours to cook, the scalloped potatoes may be cooked at the same time.

Scalloped potatoes with onion: Add 4 oz (100 g) finely chopped or grated onions to the potatoes. Cheese and/or capers may also be added.

SAVOURY POTATO FLAKY CAKE

as a frypan   *serves* 2

The potato cake will be crispy and golden brown on both sides with a savoury mixture inside. Tomatoes may be fried at the same time to make a tasty, economical meal.

8 oz (225 g) potatoes, peeled
1 medium-sized onion, peeled
salt and pepper

1 tablespoon oil or other fat for
  frying
Filling (see below)
tomatoes (optional)

1 Grate the potato and onion on a coarse grater. Add salt and pepper and mix well.
2 Put oil or fat into Cooker and set heat at moderately hot, about 300–340 (3–4).
3 Prepare the filling.
4 When fat is very hot, put half the potato and onion mixture into the Cooker and push into a neat round pile, about 6 in (15 cm) across. Cover with the savoury mixture, then top with the rest of the potato and onion. Press it down, trying to keep the shape as neat as possible. The pressing will help to make it cake together. Cook for about 7–8 minutes, or until browned underneath.
5 To make it easier to turn over, first cut in half and use a fish slice for turning. Cook for the same time on the other side. Halved, skinned tomatoes could be put in the Cooker about 5 minutes before the cake will be cooked.

FILLINGS

Grated cheese and ham: Use about 2–3 oz (50–75 g) chopped ham and about 3 oz (75 g) grated cheese. A few capers or chopped gherkins would give piquancy.

Cooked flaked fish: Spread first potato layer with 4 oz (100 g) fish and add something extra such as a tablespoon of cooked green peas or beans or mixed frozen vegetables. Season well.

Cooked chicken and ham: Use 4 oz (100 g), in any proportion. Slice and place between potato layers.

FRIED MINTED CARROTS WITH YOGHURT

as a frypan   *serves 3–4*

When fried and minted, the carrots lie in a bed of yoghurt. A dish that could be added to your vegetarian collection.

2 tablespoons butter or margarine
1 lb (½ kg) carrots, ready cooked,
    either canned or fresh
a little flour, salted

5 fl oz (150 ml) natural yoghurt
1 tablespoon chopped mint
1 tablespoon brown sugar

1 Put butter or margarine into Cooker and heat to 380 (5).
2 Dry carrots with kitchen paper and roll in flour seasoned with salt.
3 Put the yoghurt on to a shallow serving dish and warm through. This could be done by placing the dish under the Cooker.
4 When fat is very hot, fry the carrots until lightly browned, about 5 minutes.
5 When carrots are ready, sprinkle generously with chopped mint and sprinkle very lightly with brown sugar. Lift on to the bed of yoghurt.

Fried parsnips with chives and chervil: Use cooked parsnips, halved, or quartered if they are large. At step 5 sprinkle well with a mixture of finely chopped chives and dried chervil, then put on to the bed of warm yoghurt.

Fried sweet potatoes (or kumaras) with marshmallows: Use sweet potatoes or kumaras cut into 1 in (2·5 cm) slices. When fried put into a heated dish then dot the top with marshmallows. Put under the hot grill for a few minutes until the marshmallows have melted and run over the potatoes. Serve yoghurt separately.

STUFFED GREEN PEPPERS

as an oven   *serves 4*

The size of the green peppers will depend on whether they are to be served as the main part of a meal or merely as a starter.

4 small or medium-sized green   *Stuffing* (see below)
peppers

1 Slice off stem ends of peppers and remove the stems, leaving a ring. Save this ring for final garnish. Cut out seeds and membrane.
2 Rinse peppers and put into a saucepan of boiling, salted water for 3 minutes, then drain.
3 Put rack in Cooker and turn heat to 380 (5). Place a shallow heatproof dish (a freezer foil dish would do) on the rack.
4 Small or medium-sized peppers should stand up evenly. If any do lean, cut a slice off the bottom so that they stand upright. Larger peppers should be halved lengthwise.
5 Fill peppers with stuffing and stand on dish in Cooker. Top each with the sliced-off ring. (Half a ring only for any peppers you have halved.)
6 Cover with Cooker lid and open vent. Allow 20 minutes.

STUFFINGS

(quantities for 2 large or 4 small peppers)

Minced meat, onion and breadcrumbs: Fry 8 oz (225 g) minced meat with 1 medium-sized onion, chopped finely or minced. Add 4 tablespoons fresh breadcrumbs, a little salt and pepper, and $\frac{1}{2}$ teaspoon thyme. Fill peppers and top with dry breadcrumbs. Cooked rice could replace the fresh breadcrumbs.

Fish, cheese and rice: Mash 6 oz (175 g) cooked, boned fish with 3 oz (75 g) grated or cream cheese and 4 tablespoons cooked rice. If no rice is at hand use fresh breadcrumbs. Season well, fill peppers and top with dry breadcrumbs.

Rice, cheese and tomato: Mix 4 heaped tablespoons cooked rice, 3 oz (75 g) grated or cream cheese and 2 skinned, sliced tomatoes. Season well, fill peppers and top with dry breadcrumbs.

CABBAGE SAVOURY CRISP

New ways with vegetable dishes are always welcome. For a quickly-made after-work meal, three parts could be made beforehand: the hard-boiled eggs, the cheese sauce and the breadcrumb mixture.

2 eggs
¼ lb (225 g) white cabbage, washed and shredded
salt and pepper
¼ pint (150 ml) milk
1 rounded tablespoon packet soup-mix, mushroom, celery, asparagus or leek, with 3 extra tablespoons milk

2 oz (50 g), or more, tasty cheese, grated
2 or 3 tomatoes, peeled and sliced
1 teaspoon sugar
3 heaped tablespoons fresh breadcrumbs, mixed with 2 level tablespoons melted butter or margarine

1 Put eggs on to boil for about 15 minutes.
2 Put casserole dish into Cooker and turn to 420 (6).
3 Put cabbage into colander and pour hot or boiling water through. Tip into casserole and sprinkle with salt and pepper.
4 Heat the milk and stir in the soup mix mixed with the extra milk. Cook and stir until thick. Remove from the heat and add cheese.
5 Shell eggs, chop, and sprinkle over the cabbage. Pour the sauce over. Arrange tomatoes on top and sprinkle with sugar.
6 Spoon over buttered crumbs. Cover with lid and open vent. Reduce heat to 380 (5) and allow 25–30 minutes.

Cauliflower savoury crisp: Replace cabbage with cauliflower broken into florets and parboiled.

Broccoli savoury crisp: Replace cabbage with parboiled broccoli.

Celery and leek savoury crisp: Replace cabbage with 2 medium leeks and 3 sticks of celery, both chopped and parboiled.

Cocktail Party Savouries

PRUNE AND BACON ROLLS

as a frypan   *makes 16*

Cut rinds from ½ lb (225 g) streaky bacon, then cut each rasher into 2 pieces, each 4–4½ in (10·5 cm) long. Put 1 stoned, cooked prune on each piece and roll up. Secure with cocktail sticks, one for each. While doing this, put 2 teaspoons lard or butter into Cooker and heat to 300 (3). When light goes out, brush Cooker with the fat and fry the rolls for a few minutes on either side. If they have been made beforehand, they can be reheated in the Cooker: put a shallow cake tin or a sheet of foil on the rack and turn heat to 340 (4). Cover with lid and open vent. Allow to heat through without cooking any more. Serve at once.

Note: The prunes may first be soaked in port wine or sherry.

Angels on horseback: Follow the recipe above for Prune and Bacon Rolls, using uncooked bearded oysters instead of the prunes. The oysters could be sprinkled with a few drops of lemon juice. Reheat gently and not for too long or the oysters will toughen.

CHEESE AND CHIVE ROLLED CRISPS

as a frypan   *makes 12*

Allow 3 good tablespoons cream cheese and mix with a little mayonnaise or salad cream to moisten. Add 1 tablespoon chopped chives and season with salt and pepper. Put 2 tablespoons butter or margarine into Cooker and turn to 300 (3). Have 12 thin-cut pieces of white bread 2 in (5 cm) wide and 4½ in (11·25 cm) long, crusts removed. Spread with the cheese mixture and roll up. If ends are pressed firmly, cocktail sticks will not be necessary. Fry in the hot fat until lightly browned and crisp. Raise heat a little if frying too slowly. Serve hot.

Smoked roe and cheese rolled crisps: Instead of the cheese and chive mixture, mash a 1 in (2·5 cm) slice of smoked roe with 2 good tablespoons cream cheese. Add 2 teaspoons lemon juice.

CHEESE PUFF TARTLETS

makes 10

These may be made several days before the party and reheated just before the guests arrive.

6 oz (175 g) short pastry,
    bought or homemade (p. 193)
1 egg
4 oz (100 g) tasty Cheddar or
    Parmesan cheese, grated

6 tablespoons milk
salt and pepper
seasoning salt or monosodium
    glutamate

1 Roll out the pastry thinly, then cut into 3½–4 in (9·5 cm) rounds and fit into pattypans or foil baking cases, pressing down firmly. Mark edges with a fork to decorate.
2 Put rack in Cooker and turn to 420 (6). Leave for 5 minutes then put in the pans. Cover with lid and open vent. Allow 15 minutes.
3 Beat the egg and add cheese, milk and seasonings. Lift lid and pour mixture into the half-cooked pastry cases. Cover again. Reduce heat to 380 (5) and cook for 15 minutes. Serve hot.

LITTLE FISH BALLS

as a frypan *makes 16–18*

½ lb (225 g) cooked fish, skinned
    and boned
3 oz (75 g) smoked roe or smoked
    fish
2 oz (50 g) fresh breadcrumbs
1 egg, beaten

2 teaspoons anchovy essence
2 tablespoons oil, butter or
    margarine
milk
fine dry breadcrumbs

1 Combine the fish—both sorts—fresh breadcrumbs, egg and anchovy essence.
2 Put fat into Cooker and turn to 340 (4).
3 Form mixture into 1 in (2·5 cm) balls. Dip into milk then into breadcrumbs and fry until golden. Put on to cocktail sticks and serve hot.

TOAST BASKETS

as an oven

These crisp little 'baskets' are useful for holding savoury mixtures for cocktail parties and make a change from pastry. They can also be filled with cooked peas and used as an attractive garnish around a roast.

$3\frac{1}{2}$ in (9 cm) squares of thin-cut
    bread
melted butter

Savoury Fillings (see below) *or*
    cooked green peas

1 Put rack in Cooker and heat to 420 (6).
2 Use deep pattypans or small freezer foil baking cases (the tartlet cases are a little too small).
3 Brush the bread squares with melted butter on one side only.
4 Press squares into cases, buttered side down. Place on rack, cover with Cooker lid and open vent.
5 Bake for about 15–20 minutes, or until crisp and golden.
6 Fill either with savoury fillings for cocktail parties, or with cooked green peas for a garnish around a roast. Reheat before serving.

SAVOURY FILLINGS

Chicken and ham: Make either Cream Sauce (*p. 189*) or a packet soup-mix sauce, any flavour. Stir in about 4 oz (100 g) chicken and 4 oz (100 g) ham, both minced, or ground in blender. Fill baskets, top with sprigs of parsley or slices of stuffed olives. Will fill 20–22 baskets.

Bacon and egg: Remove rinds from 3 rashers of streaky bacon and cut into $\frac{1}{2}$ in (1·25 cm) pieces. Fry either in Cooker or a smaller pan. Beat 2 eggs and add 4 tablespoons milk. Add salt and pepper and seasoning salt. Add to bacon and cook gently until scrambled. Fill baskets and garnish with parsley sprigs or slices of stuffed olives. Will fill 16 baskets.

2

Meats
Poultry and Game
Sausage, Liver and Kidney Dishes

In the majority of these recipes the Multi Cooker replaces the conventional oven and so saves expensive heating costs. It also allows those with tiny kitchens to extend their cooking repertoire to include roasts with roast potatoes and all the popular casserole dishes. Many recipes are called 'Cook-and-Serve Dishes'. These are cooked directly in the Cooker and may be served from it. Long slow cooking is also included.

ROAST BEEF

as an oven

For roasting, choose either boned rolled sirloin or other prime ribs or wing rib on the bone. These joints may be underdone to any degree desired and still be tender and succulent. All have some fat running through and this enhances the flavour. Topside, brisket and silverside are only suitable for pot-roasting.

2 good tablespoons beef dripping or other fat
roasting joint of beef, any size (see above)
flour

salt and pepper
potatoes and any other root vegetables, peeled, for roasting
gravy (p. 190)

1 Put fat into Cooker and turn heat to 380 (5).
2 Wipe meat and dust with flour. Sprinkle with salt and pepper.
3 When fat is hot, brown meat on one side only.
4 Put vegetables into boiling, salted water for 5 minutes, then drain well.
5 Lift out meat and place in Cooker a 6½ in (16 cm) piece of foil or small rack, upside down and so almost touching floor of Cooker. Place meat on the rack or foil, browned side up, and arrange the vegetables in the fat on the floor of the Cooker. Turn vegetables to coat with fat and sprinkle with salt and pepper.
6 Cover with Cooker lid and open vent. Reduce heat to 340 (4) or a little less. Cooking should be fairly brisk, without danger of burning. Baste after 30 minutes and turn vegetables.
7 Allow the following cooking times:
    Boned and rolled roast: rare—20 minutes per lb (½ kg) and 20 minutes extra; *medium rare*—24 minutes per lb (½ kg) and 24 minutes extra; *well done*—27 minutes per lb (½ kg) and 27 minutes extra.
    Wing rib on the bone: subtract 2 minutes per lb (½ kg) from the above times.
8 When meat is cooked, remove and make gravy, p. 190.

BOEUF À LA MODE

as a large saucepan

This is a variation of the popular pot roast. It gets its grand name because, unlike its plain-Jane cousin, it is first marinated in a delicious combination of flavours.

2–4 lb (1–2 kg) topside, fresh
    brisket or silverside
1 tablespoon oil or cooking fat
2 pints (1 litre) water
salt and pepper
root vegetables, such as potatoes
    parsnips and carrots, peeled
    and cut, and whole onions,
    peeled

MARINADE
½ pint (275 ml) red wine with the
    same amount of water, or
    1 pint (575 ml) cider or ale
1 onion, peeled and halved
1 bouquet garni or 1 teaspoon
    mixed herbs
1 well-crushed clove of garlic, or
    use garlic salt or powder
4 cloves

1 Put all marinade ingredients into a deep bowl and place meat in it. Baste with the liquid and leave for 4 or more hours, turning meat twice.
2 When meat is ready, put oil or fat into Cooker and turn heat to 380 (5) until very hot. Dab meat dry (reserve marinade for the broth) and fry on both sides until browned.
3 Add water and a little salt and pepper.
4 When water begins to boil, reduce to simmering and cover with Cooker lid. Close vent.
5 Cook for 1 hour then pour in the marinade and continue cooking for another hour.
6 Add the root vegetables and continue to simmer, adding more water if it is boiling too much. There should be at least 2 pints (1 litre) of broth at the end. Some of the broth may be thickened to make a gravy.

Cooking times: Judge time by the thickness of the meat. 2½–3 in (7 cm) thick, allow 3 hours; 3½–4 in (9 cm) thick, allow 3½–4 hours.

Pot au feu: The recipe may be treated as a Pot au feu, that is, the broth may be strained and served as a consommé (with some fat removed), with the meat and vegetables following as the main course.

PEGGY'S ARGENTINIAN STEAK (1)
(casserole)

as an oven   *serves 3–4*

Keen, strong palates will enjoy this South American dish. Peggy says that she makes double or treble the quantity and puts several containers of it in her deep freeze.

2 rashers of streaky bacon
1 tablespoon margarine
¾–1 lb (350–450 g) stewing steak
1 large onion, peeled and chopped
2 level tablespoons flour
1 teaspoon curry powder
2 tablespoons tomato ketchup
½ teaspoon tabasco sauce
1 teaspoon ground ginger

1 teaspoon Worcester sauce
2 tablespoons brown sugar
1 tablespoon vinegar
¼ pint (150 ml) beer
salt and pepper to taste
1 or more crushed cloves of garlic,
    or 1 teaspoon garlic salt or
    powder (optional)

1 Put casserole dish in Cooker and heat to 420 (6) or maximum.
2 Cut bacon (rinds removed) into 1 in (2·5 cm) pieces. Add to casserole with the margarine. Fry until sizzling.
3 Trim meat and cut into pieces about 2 in (5 cm) square and add with the onion. Fry together for 3 minutes. Mix in flour.
4 Add curry powder, ketchup, tabasco, ginger, Worcester sauce, brown sugar, vinegar and beer. Stir all together.
5 Add seasoning and the garlic, if liked.
6 Leave on high heat until gravy begins to bubble, then cover with casserole lid and Cooker lid. Close vent.
7 Reduce heat to 300 (3) or gently boiling. Have a look after about 45 minutes and if boiling too fast reduce heat to 260 (2). Allow about 2½ hours. Meats such as bladebone, chuck or rump steak should take only about 2 hours.

Peggy's Argentinian steak (2) (as a cook-and-serve dish): To make the dish directly in the Cooker, put margarine and bacon into Cooker, turn to 340 (4) and fry. Add onions and meat and fry for 3 minutes. Add all other ingredients except flour and add 1 pint (575 ml) water, or part beer. Cover and close vent. Cook at about 220 (1) and simmer gently. Add more water if necessary and thicken at the end.

BRAISED STEAK (2)
(casserole)

This method may of course be used for 4 or more servings, using a large casserole (see introduction on p. 68).

¾–1 lb (350–500 g) stewing steak
1 tablespoon oil or other cooking fat
1 onion, peeled and chopped, or use frozen chopped onions
1 level dessertspoon flour
1 crushed clove of garlic, or use garlic salt or powder (optional)

¼ pint (150 ml) water
1 beef stock cube
½ teaspoon thyme
1 or more carrots, cleaned and sliced
salt and pepper (2 teaspoons soy sauce may replace some of the salt)

1 The steak may be cut into 1 in (2·5 cm) cubes or into serving-size pieces, about 3 in by 4 in (7·5 cm by 10 cm). Trim if necessary.
2 Use a heatproof casserole dish that will sit comfortably in the Cooker. Enamel or metal will fry more quickly than Pyrex. Put it into Cooker and turn heat to 420 (6) or maximum.
3 Add fat and, when very hot, fry the meat until well seared.
4 Add onions and flour and fry for 3 minutes. Add garlic if liked.
5 Add the water (preferably hot), crumbled stock cube, thyme, carrots and seasoning. Stir all together.
6 When gravy begins to bubble, reduce heat to 300 (3). Cover with casserole lid then with Cooker lid and close vent.
7 Have a look after 30 minutes. If gravy is boiling too fast, reduce heat to 220 (1). For good bladebone or rump, allow 1¾–2 hours; for shin, 3 hours; and for other stewing steak, 2½ hours.

Note: Jacket potatoes may be cooking around the casserole. If so, first put a piece of foil on the floor of the Cooker and stand the casserole on it. Place the scrubbed potatoes on the foil around the dish. When cooked, hold with a towel in one hand and with the other make two slits in a cross. Press from the bottom and push up some of the potato. Put a lump of butter in the centre of each.

Braised steak (3) (long slow cooking): Follow ingredients and method for Braised Steak (2). The amounts could be increased for more servings. Do not try to bake potatoes around the dish. Make sure that the onions and carrots are very finely chopped. When the gravy begins to bubble (step 6) lift out dish and put in the rack—about $\frac{1}{4}$–$\frac{1}{2}$ in (0·5–1·25 cm)—above floor of Cooker. Reduce heat to 220 (1). Put covered dish on rack, cover with Cooker lid and close vent. Leave to cook for 7 hours at least, 8 or 9 will tenderize the meat even more. After the first hour, open up. The gravy should be just moving, neither bubbling nor completely still. Reduce heat if necessary.

VARIATIONS TO (1), (2) OR (3)

With tomatoes: Replace water with $\frac{1}{2}$ lb (225 g) peeled, sliced tomatoes. If you have increased quantities for more servings, replace $\frac{1}{4}$ pint (150 ml) of the liquid with the tomatoes. Add Worcester sauce to taste and 1 or 2 teaspoons sugar.

With mushrooms: To get the best flavour from the mushrooms, wash and slice then fry in a little butter or margarine in another frying pan. Use as a garnish.

With wine or sherry: Replace some of the water with wine or sherry: 2–3 tablespoons sherry or 4–6 tablespoons wine, preferably red.

With many vegetables: Add all or some of these: 2–3 sticks of celery; 1 large or 2 small leeks; 1 chopped deseeded green pepper and the tomatoes and mushrooms suggested above.

BEEF OLIVES

as a cook-and-serve dish or as a casserole serves 4

For generations this dish has been popular for both party and family occasions. Many variations are possible, see below.

1¼ lb (575 g) good stewing steak, beaten out very thinly by the butcher
Forcemeat Stuffing (p. 78)
1 tablespoon oil or other fat
1 medium-sized onion, peeled and chopped
1 crushed clove of garlic, or 1 teaspoon garlic salt or powder (optional)

1 pint (575 ml) hot stock or water with 1 beef stock cube (some of the water can be replaced with 5–8 tablespoons wine or 3–5 tablespoons sherry)
2 level tablespoons packet soup-mix, any flavour, or homemade roux (p. 14)
salt and pepper

1 Trim the meat if necessary and slice into pieces 4 in by 5 in (10 cm by 12·5 cm). Put 1 tablespoon stuffing on each and roll up. Secure with tiny skewers or thread.

2 Put fat into Cooker and turn heat to 340 (4) or medium frying temperature. When hot, fry rolls until lightly browned and remove to a plate.

3 Add onion and fry until transparent. Add garlic, if liked.

4 Reduce heat to simmering, and add liquid and stock cube, if used. Some of the water will boil away during cooking.

5 Put rolls back. Cover with Cooker lid and close vent.

6 Simmer gently for 1–1¼ hours, or until rolls are tender. Add more water if necessary.

7 About 10 minutes before cooking time is up, add the soup mix or roux. Taste and add salt and pepper. Stir and cook until thickened, then cover and finish the cooking.

Beef olives en casserole: Everything may be prepared in a casserole sitting in the Cooker. Place casserole in Cooker and turn heat to 420 (6). Add the fat, then brown the rolls and remove to a plate. Fry onions in the casserole and add garlic, if liked. Mix in the packet soup-mix or roux, then add half the quantity of liquid used above. Mix well, then put the rolls back. When gravy begins to bubble, reduce heat to 300 (3). Cover with casserole lid and Cooker lid and close vent. Allow 1–1¼ hours or until rolls are tender.

Beef rolls with bacon and prunes: Instead of forcemeat stuffing, put a piece of rindless bacon on each slice of meat topped with 2 cooked, stoned prunes. Roll up as for Beef Olives and proceed with the recipe.

Beef rolls with cocktail sausages: Instead of forcemeat stuffing roll each piece of meat around a cocktail sausage. Secure with cocktail sticks or tiny skewers and proceed with the recipe.

Beef rolls with liver pâté: Instead of forcemeat stuffing spread each piece of meat with liver or other pâté and roll up. Secure with cocktail sticks and proceed with the recipe.

Beef rolls with dates and almond: Instead of forcemeat stuffing spread each piece of meat with the following mixture:

Put 3 oz (75 g) chopped, stoned dates into a saucepan with 4 tablespoons water, wine or sherry. Bring to the boil, then remove from heat and mash. Stir in 1 teaspoon sugar, 1 heaped tablespoon ground almonds and $\frac{1}{2}$ teaspoon almond essence. After spreading the meat with this, roll up and secure with cocktail sticks or tiny skewers. Proceed with the recipe.

ENAIDA'S HUNGARIAN GOULASH
(casserole)

as an oven or as a long slow cooker   *serves 4–5*

Meat that needs long cooking is done more easily in a casserole sitting in the Cooker. It can stay there for several hours, with little attention, and if cooked slowly can remain for as long as 8 hours.

1 tablespoon oil or other fat	½ lb (225 g) tomatoes, peeled and sliced
¼ lb (225 g) onions, peeled and chopped	6 tablespoons water or wine
1 or 2 crushed cloves of garlic, or garlic salt or powder (optional)	salt and pepper
	1 teaspoon sugar
1 lb (½ kg) braising steak	1 green pepper, about 4 oz (100 g) deseeded and chopped
2 teaspoons mild paprika	4 oz (100 g) mushrooms, washed and sliced
1 level tablespoon flour	

1 Put casserole dish into Cooker and turn heat to 420 (6). Put fat into dish and when hot add onions and garlic, if used, and begin to fry. (A metal or enamel dish will fry more quickly than Pyrex or china.)
2 Trim the meat if necessary and cut into 1 in (2·5 cm) cubes.
3 Add meat and paprika and fry for 2 minutes. Sprinkle in the flour, stir, and cook for another 2 minutes.
4 Add tomatoes, liquid, seasoning and sugar and mix all together.
5 When gravy begins to bubble, put on casserole lid then cover with Cooker lid and close vent. Reduce heat to 300 (3) or gently boiling and allow 2½ hours. If boiling too fast, lower heat.
6 About 10 minutes before cooking is completed, add the green pepper and the mushrooms.

Jacket potatoes may be cooked around the dish. See Note, p. 69.

Long slow cooking: Chop onions very finely. At step 5, lift out casserole and put in rack. Replace casserole. When gravy begins to bubble, lower heat to 220 (1). After 30 minutes, open up and look. The gravy should just be moving to show that it is cooking. It should not bubble. Allow about 7 hours, or longer. Do not cook jacket potatoes when long slow cooking.

EXPENSIVE STEAKS

as a frypan

Tenderness is the first quality of the expensive steaks. They come from the less-used parts of the animal, as for instance the fillet, which is more of a cushion than a muscle. Ribs such as sirloin, porterhouse, T-bone and wing ribs are working muscles, but they do not have the heavy work demanded of them as do the legs and shoulders, therefore they are tender enough to be roasted, fried or grilled. They also have the virtue of being tender and delicious when underdone. No other meats can compete here.

See p. 76 for tenderized 'supermarket' steaks.

FILLET STEAKS

Tournedos: Round fillet steaks cut into 1–1½ in (3 cm) slices. To cook, put 2 teaspoons oil or butter into Cooker and turn heat to 340 (4). Sprinkle the meat with salt and pepper and, if liked, a little garlic powder. Wait until light goes out and fat is very hot; fry as follows:

1 in (2·5 cm) thick: rare—1½ minutes on each side; *medium rare*—2½ minutes on each side; *well done*—3 minutes on each side.

1½ in (3·75 cm) thick: rare—2 minutes on each side; *medium rare*—3 minutes on each side; *well done*—3½–4 minutes on each side.

Each steak may be topped with a square of Maître d'Hôtel Butter (*p. 191*). If gravy is needed, see Wine Gravy (*p. 190*).

Tournedos Rossini: Follow frying times for Tournedos, above. Warm slices of pâté de foie gras, or other liver pâté, about the size of the steaks. Keep hot on a plate. When steaks are cooked, top each with a piece of the pâté. Garnish with slices of stuffed olives. See Wine Gravy (*p. 190*), using Madeira.

Filet mignon: Cut from the thinner end of the fillet and 1½ in (3·75 cm) thick. Before frying the steaks, fry pieces of bread cut about the same size as the fillets, using extra fat. Keep hot. Skin some large tomatoes and cut into 1 in (2·5 cm) slices. Place at one end of the Cooker and sprinkle with salt and pepper and a little sugar. Fry the steaks as suggested for the 1½ in (3·75 cm) thick Tournedos, above. Serve each steak on a piece of fried bread and top with a slice of tomato. See Wine Gravy (*p. 190*).

Minute steaks: Fillet steaks cut $\frac{1}{2}-\frac{3}{4}$ in (1·5 cm) thick. Fry as for Tournedos, above, but allow only $\frac{1}{2}$ minute on each side.

Châteaubriand: Very expensive, very thick, very large. It is cut from the centre of the fillet and is about $2-2\frac{1}{2}$ in (5·5 cm) thick. It usually weighs about 14 oz (400 g) and will serve 2–3 people. First fry at 340 (4) for 2 minutes on each side to brown, then lower heat to 300 (3) or a little lower and fry for another 8–12 minutes, depending on thickness and choice of finish.

PORTERHOUSE STEAKS

Cut from the wing ribs and usually $1-1\frac{1}{2}$ in (3 cm) thick. They have a better flavour than the fillet steaks. Fry as for Tournedos (*p. 74*) but allow the following times:

1 in (2·5 cm) thick: rare—2 minutes on each side; *medium rare*— $3\frac{1}{2}$ minutes on each side; *well done*—6 minutes on each side.

1$\frac{1}{2}$ in (3·75 cm) thick: rare—4 minutes on each side; *medium rare*— 5 minutes on each side; *well done*—6 minutes on each side.

Serve just with the drippings from the pan poured over, with plain gravy or with Wine Gravy (*p. 190*).

T-BONE STEAKS

Cut from the sirloin. The bone is in the shape of a T, having a piece of fillet on one side and a piece of sirloin on the other. Fry as for porterhouse steaks, above, and serve in the same way.

SIRLOIN STEAKS

Fine-flavoured steaks cut from the sirloin bone. Fry as for porterhouse steaks, above, but allow 2 more minutes on each side.

'SUPERMARKET' STEAKS

as a frypan

When the purse has to be stretched to meet the family's large appetites or the Income Tax man has just taken his whack, the supermarkets, as well as some butchers, offer a variety of grilling steaks that are tenderized in various ways and yet are inexpensive. Some may be made to resemble those upper-crust steaks that grace the previous two pages (supermarkets usually sell these too, which is a sign of an affluent society).

SEASONED BEEF GRILLS

These are made from minced beef, pleasantly flavoured and flattened into rectangular or square 'steaks'. To pan-fry, put 1 tablespoon oil, margarine or other fat into the Cooker and turn heat to 380 (5). When fat is very hot, fry the steaks for $\frac{1}{2}$ minute on each side. If you prefer them well done continue frying at 340 (4) for 2 more minutes on each side. See below for accompaniments.

QUICK FRY, FLASH FRY, BEEF TENDER STEAKS

These are the names given by various stores to their steaks. They come from cuts such as bladebone, shoulder, topside, chuck, clod and thick skirt. They are neatly shaped to resemble the expensive steaks, then tenderized in a machine designed for the purpose. They emerge with a cross-stitch effect. Fry them in the same way as seasoned beef grills, above.

Accompaniments
Gravy or Wine Gravy (*p. 190*).
Fried bread and tomato slices to make mock Filets Mignons (*p. 74*).
Liver pâté, see Tournedos Rossini (*p. 74*).
Fried mushrooms and skinned, halved tomatoes: Begin to fry washed mushrooms at one end of the pan before frying steaks. Add the tomatoes to the mushrooms and heat through.
Maître d'Hotel Butter (*p. 191*).

DEVILLED MARINATED STEAKS

as a frypan

Gives a distinct lift to 'supermarket' steaks, and can also enhance the more expensive ones.

4 frying steaks (see pp. 74–6)
1 tablespoon oil or fat

DEVIL
2 tablespoons vinegar
1 tablespoon soft brown sugar
3 tablespoons water
3 teaspoons Worcester sauce

2 teaspoons tomato purée
1 teaspoon mixed mustard
  (optional)
½ teaspoon seasoning salt or
  herb-and-spice salt
a little pepper
½–1 teaspoon garlic powder
  (optional)

1 Mix together all the ingredients for the 'devil'.
2 Put steaks on to a plate or other shallow dish. Pour the 'devil' over and leave for 2 or more hours or overnight.
3 Put fat or oil into Cooker and heat to 340 (4).
4 Lift steaks from the 'devil' and shake free of surplus.
5 Fry for the times suggested for the different steaks on pp. 74–6.
6 Lift out steaks and pour in the 'devil' liquid. When hot, pour over the steaks. Serve with any of the accompaniments suggested for the other steaks.

Saintly Marinated Steaks

Saintly marinade (1): Combine the juice of 1 lemon with 1 teaspoon sugar, 2 tablespoons water, 1 teaspoon celery or onion salt (or half of each), 1 bay leaf broken into 3 pieces and, if liked, ½–1 teaspoon garlic powder. Continue from step 2 above.

Saintly marinade (2): Combine 3 tablespoons of red wine or 2 of sherry; 3 tablespoons water (4 if sherry is used); 1 teaspoon soy sauce or ½ crumbled beef stock cube; 1 bay leaf broken into 3 pieces; ½–1 teaspoon garlic powder, if liked. Continue from step 2 above.

RUMP STEAK AND ONIONS

as a frypan   *serves 2–3*

This is an expensive steak but as it is different from the others on
pp. 74–5 it needs a separate recipe. Only if cut well into the centre
can rump be underdone. Here it is fried until browned, then cooked
slowly until tender.

1 lb (½ kg) rump steak   *garlic powder (optional)*
  about 1¼ in (3 cm) thick   *2 large onions, peeled and*
1 level tablespoon oil or other fat   *chopped*
salt and pepper   *1 pint (575 ml) water*

1 If you wish, trim a little of the fat from the rump; but I find this
   unnecessary as it is such delicious fat.
2 Put oil or other fat into Cooker and turn heat to 340 (4).
3 When light has gone out, put in the meat and fry for 2 or 3 minutes
   until browned on one side. Turn over and baste with the fat.
   Sprinkle with salt and pepper and, if liked, a little garlic powder.
4 Reduce heat down to 220 (1) or gently sizzling. Cover with
   Cooker lid and close vent. Leave for 15 minutes.
5 Open up and turn and baste again, then add onions. Fry for 5–8
   minutes, or until browned. Add water. This will boil down. Add a
   little salt and pepper. Cover again with vent closed and simmer
   for about 1 hour or until meat is tender. Baste during cooking and
   add more water when necessary.

Stuffed rump steak: Buy a neat piece about 1½ in (3·75 cm) thick.
Ask the butcher to cut a pocket in the side. Fill this with either
Forcemeat Stuffing (below) or with 2 in (5 cm) pieces of fried bacon
and mushrooms. Onions may be included if wished. Fry and simmer
as suggested in the recipe, allowing 1½ hours for the final simmering.
Add extra water if boiling off unduly.

Forcemeat Stuffing: Mix 2 oz (50 g or 1 cup) fresh breadcrumbs
with ½ small onion, grated (or 1 teaspoon dried onion flakes); ½ teaspoon thyme or mixed herbs; ¼ teaspoon salt and a little pepper;
1 dessertspoon chopped parsley. Chop in roughly 2 teaspoons butter.

SETSUKO'S SUKI YAKI

This traditional Japanese dish is always cooked on the table with guests sitting around. The Multi Cooker is the ideal vessel for this. The recipes vary greatly, as for all traditional dishes. This one was given to me by an excellent Japanese cook married to a New Zealander. The ingredients may be varied according to taste and availability. The Japanese use long chopsticks for cooking Suki Yaki but food tongs are easier. There should be two bowls by each guest, one for rice and the other, usually with a raw egg in it, for the Suki Yaki. Guests may use either the small Japanese chopsticks or, for the inexpert, a spoon.

3 large carrots, cleaned
½ small mild cabbage
½ lb (225 g) cauliflower florets
  and/or ½ lb (225 g) mushrooms,
  sliced
½ lb (225 g), or less, bamboo
  shoots
1 bunch spring onions, trimmed
2 large onions, peeled
1½ lb (¾ kg) porterhouse steak,
  very thinly sliced: cut either by
  the butcher on a bacon slicer,
  or at home, chilled before
  slicing
1 lb (450 g) bean curd, cut into
  small squares, or slimming
  bread rolls, soaked and
  squeezed
2 oz (50 g) fine Chinese-type
  vermicelli

4 rounded tablespoons sugar
2 oz (50 g) butter
salt and pepper

SAUCE
10 tablespoons Japanese soy
  sauce (shoyu), or 6 tablespoons
  Chinese soy sauce (Japanese is
  preferable)
10 tablespoons chicken stock or
  sake (Japanese rice wine) or a
  medium dry sherry
1 level teaspoon monosodium
  glutamate (optional)

FOR THE BOWLS
4 raw eggs
2 lb (1 kg), or 4 large cups,
  boiled rice

1 Slice carrots into thin discs and blanch in hot water for a few minutes, then drain and rinse in cold water to preserve the colour. Do the same with the cabbage, cauliflower florets, mushrooms, bamboo shoots and spring onions.

2 Dice the onions, then cut the meat into bite-sized pieces.

3 Arrange all these ingredients in neat piles on one or two trays. Have handy the sugar, the butter, the ingredients for the sauce

mixed together in a jug, and salt and pepper for those who may like it.

4 To cook the Suki Yaki, put the butter in Cooker and turn to 420 (6). When butter is melted add half the diced onions. When they are transparent push them to one end of the Cooker.

5 Now add half the meat and brown on both sides. Then sprinkle half the sugar on the meat and pour over half the sauce. Stir until simmering. Move the meat next to the onions.

6 Add some of each of the other ingredients and simmer in the sauce for 5 minutes.

7 The guests break the eggs into their bowls and beat them with their chopsticks. When the hot food is added, the egg will be slightly cooked. The hostess puts a serving into the bowls containing the egg then fills the other bowls with rice. After that the guests help themselves from the Cooker in the middle of the table.

8 Cooking is continuous. While the first serving is being eaten, more ingredients are added to the Cooker, with more sugar on the meat, and more sauce to continue the simmering. The sauce becomes more and more delicious and can be spooned on to the rice towards the end.

9 Serve with Chinese tea, white wine or warm *sake*. Finish with fresh fruit.

STRIPED MEAT LOAF

When the loaf is turned out, the reddish-yellow layer will be in the middle of the meat layers giving an attractive striped effect. A fine-flavoured party piece, either hot or cold, and a picnic special.

MEAT LAYERS (see Note)
1 lb (½ kg) lean beef, minced
1 medium-sized onion, peeled and grated or finely chopped
2 oz (50 g) fresh breadcrumbs
1 level teaspoon thyme
2 teaspoons concentrated tomato purée
1 teaspoon sugar
1 standard egg, beaten
salt and pepper

CARROT AND CHEESE LAYER
½ lb (225 g) carrots, scraped and grated
4 oz (100 g) bright yellow Cheddar cheese, grated
1½ oz (38 g) fresh breadcrumbs
1 standard egg, beaten
1 level teaspoon dried sage
salt and pepper

1 Use a loaf tin about 4½ in by 8½ in (11·25 cm by 21·25 cm) and if not non-stick, grease well. A freezer foil loaf tin would do.
2 Combine all the ingredients for the meat layers and set aside.
3 Put rack in Cooker and turn heat to 420 (6). Cover with lid while heating.
4 Combine all the ingredients for the carrot and cheese layer.
5 Put half the meat mixture into the loaf tin and press down evenly and firmly.
6 Cover with all the carrot–cheese mixture and press down evenly.
7 Put in the rest of the meat mixture; press evenly and cover with foil.
8 Place on rack and cover with Cooker lid. Open vent. After 15 minutes reduce heat to 340 (4). Allow 1¼ hours.
9 Turn out.

Note: If this loaf is too large for your needs, halve the ingredients and cook in a smaller loaf tin, 3¾ in by 7½ in (9·5 cm by 18·75 cm). You could make the smaller one a double- instead of a triple-layered loaf. Put the meat in first, then the carrot and cheese mixture on top.

Beefburgers and Relations

as a frypan

The beefburger and its relations cover a wide range of pan-fried meat cakes. In days of old, anything that was caked together was called a 'cake', thus Shrewsbury Cakes, which today we call 'biscuits'. Still left over from those days are the 'fish cake' and the 'potato cake'.

BASIC BEEFBURGER

Allow 4 oz (100 g) minced lean beef for each person. Put 1 or 2 tablespoons oil or other cooking fat into Cooker and set heat at 340 (4) or a good frying temperature. Sprinkle beef with salt and pepper and form into flat cakes. When fat is very hot fry them for about 2 or 3 minutes on one side then turn, flatten a little with the blade of a knife, or use a fish slice, and cook for another 2 or 3 minutes. If you like them well done, allow 5–6 minutes. Tomatoes, skinned and halved, or washed sliced mushrooms could be cooking at the same time. Serve the beefburgers as they are or between horizontally sliced baps. Usually served with pickles.

Beefburger with onion: For each 8 oz (225 g) minced beef add 1 small minced or finely grated onion.

Beefburger with bacon: This is easy if you mince your own beef. Allow 1 bacon rasher for each 8 oz (225 g) of beef and mince together. Onion could be minced in at the same time.

Beefburger with soy sauce: Replace the salt with soy sauce. Allow 2 teaspoons for each 8 oz (225 g) minced beef.

Beefburger with tomato purée: Add 2 teaspoons tomato purée and 1 level teaspoon sugar for each 8 oz (225 g) beef. A little Worcester sauce could also be added.

NATIONWIDE MEATBALLS

Many nations have their traditional meatballs. There are German, Italian, Swedish, Hungarian meatballs and many others; we start with a British version.

1 lb (½ kg) minced beef
2 oz (50 g) fresh breadcrumbs
1 medium-sized onion, peeled and finely chopped or minced
1 egg, beaten
3 tablespoons milk
¼ teaspoon thyme
1 teaspoon salt and a little pepper
2 tablespoons oil or fat

GRAVY
1 pint (575 ml) water
1 medium-sized onion, peeled and chopped
1 beef stock cube
2 tomatoes, peeled and sliced
¼ teaspoon sugar
salt and pepper
¼ teaspoon basil
1 level tablespoon homemade roux (p. 14) or packet soup-mix

1 Combine mince, breadcrumbs, onion, beaten egg, milk, thyme and seasoning.
2 Put fat in Cooker and turn to 340 (4).
3 Form mixture into 2 in (5 cm) balls, roll in flour and fry in the hot fat until browned all over. Reduce heat to simmer.
4 To make gravy, add water, onion, crumbled stock cube, tomatoes, sugar, salt and pepper and basil.
5 Cover with lid and close vent. Simmer for 30 minutes.
6 Lift meatballs into a hot serving dish and keep warm.
7 Thicken gravy with homemade roux or packet soup-mix. Cook and stir until thickened.

German meatballs: Use ½ lb (225 g) minced beef, ¼ lb (100 g) minced veal and ¼ lb (100 g) minced pigs' liver.

Italian meatballs: Use minced beef and add 1 or more crushed cloves of garlic, 2 tablespoons grated Parmesan cheese and 2 tablespoons finely chopped, deseeded sweet red peppers.

Swedish meatballs: Use 6 oz (175 g) cooked rice instead of the breadcrumbs.

Hungarian meatballs: Instead of the beef use ½ lb (225 g) minced veal and ½ lb (225 g) minced pork. Add 2–4 teaspoons mild paprika.

MEAT RISSOLES

as a frypan   *makes 6–7*

Hot on Sunday, cold on Monday, rissoles on Tuesday. That was the usual pattern in the days when joints were inexpensive and large. Today we cut our cloth closer to the stitching, leaving little for Monday and nothing for Tuesday. But in winter, rissoles are more acceptable than cold meat and the Cooker fries them perfectly.

about 12 oz (350 g) left-over meat from the joint
1 onion, peeled and quartered
6 oz (175 g) mashed potatoes, fresh-cooked or dried (or left-over)
1 level teaspoon salt and a little pepper (or replace the salt with 2 teaspoons soy sauce)

1 level teaspoon thyme
1 egg, beaten
1 tablespoon chopped parsley (optional)
2 tablespoons oil or other cooking fat
flour or fine dry breadcrumbs or wheatgerm

1 Mince or blend together the meat and onion.
2 Tip into a bowl and add potato, seasoning, thyme, beaten egg and, if available, the parsley. Mix well.
3 Put oil or fat into Cooker and bring to 340 (4).
4 Form mixture into flat round cakes about ¾ in (2 cm) thick and 3 in (7·5 cm) across. Cover with either flour, fine dry breadcrumbs or wheatgerm.
5 When light has gone out and fat is very hot, fry the rissoles for 4–5 minutes on each side or until browned. Do not cover with cooker lid.

Chicken and ham rissoles: Use any proportion of cooked chicken and ham, omitting soy sauce.

Turkey and ham rissoles: Use any proportion of cooked turkey and ham, omitting soy sauce.

Fish rissoles: See Fish Cakes on p. 32, with variation.

ROAST LAMB

as an oven

Take no notice of those who say that lamb should be pink in the middle. It's not true. To get the full flavour and right texture it must be cooked slowly and thoroughly until tender. Half-cooked lamb means only half the lamb's savour. Note the addition of sugar to the fat; it helps to brown the gravy.

2 tablespoons dripping or other fat (more fat will come from the joint)
joint of lamb, any suitable size

potatoes, peeled, for roasting
1 teaspoon sugar
salt and pepper
gravy (p. 190)

1 Put fat into Cooker and heat to 380 (5).
2 When very hot, brown lamb well on one side only. Lift out.
3 Meanwhile, put the potatoes in boiling, salted water for 5 minutes. Drain well.
4 Place a small rack, about 6½ in (16 cm) across, upside down (so that it almost touches the base) in Cooker. Put meat on this, browned side up. Sprinkle the sugar into the fat. Arrange potatoes around meat on the floor of Cooker and turn to coat with fat. Sprinkle with salt and pepper.
5 Cover with lid and open vent. Reduce heat to 300 (3) or less. The fat must sizzle only very gently.
6 Allow 35 minutes per lb (½ kg) and 35 minutes extra. Turn potatoes every 30 minutes.
7 Lift out lamb and potatoes. Spoon off fat, leaving the residue. Make gravy.

Stuffed, boned shoulder of lamb: Ask the butcher to bone the shoulder ready for stuffing. Make Forcemeat Stuffing (*p. 78*) or the Roast Chicken Stuffing on p. 105. Fill opening and secure with cocktail sticks or thread. Roast as above.

BRAISED LEG OF LAMB À LA CUILLÈRE

as a casserole

'When braised,' said one famous French chef, 'lamb should be so tender that it can be served with a spoon.' This is achieved by slow cooking and frequent basting.

2 lb (1 kg) or more, thick end of leg of lamb
2 medium-sized onions
2 or 3 sticks of celery, trimmed and chopped, or if out of season use 1 leek

1 medium-sized carrot
2 tablespoons oil or other fat
1 bouquet garni
1¼ pints (850 ml) water
salt and pepper

1 Wash and dry meat. Trim if necessary.
2 Prepare vegetables; peel onions and carrot but leave them whole.
3 Put fat into Cooker and turn heat to 340 (4). When sizzling, add vegetables. Fry for 2 minutes, then put in the meat and brown it on both sides.
4 Add bouquet garni and water. Season with 1 teaspoon salt and a little pepper. Baste.
5 Reduce heat to below 220 (1). Cover with Cooker lid and close vent.
6 Cook very gently, allowing the water to simmer only. Baste now and again and add more water if necessary. Don't let it go below about 1 pint (575 ml). Cook a 2 lb (1 kg) joint for 2 hours and a 2½–3 lb (1¼–1½ kg) joint for 2½ hours.
7 Take out meat and vegetables and keep hot. Tip Cooker slightly and let gravy run to one end. When fat rises to the top, spoon some of it off. The rest may be thickened with 1–2 tablespoons home-made roux (*p. 14*), packet soup-mix or potato powder, depending on how thick you like your gravy. Purée vegetables and add to gravy.

Note: Peeled whole potatoes could be boiling in the water around the meat. Allow about 45 minutes, depending on size.

BRIGHTON MARINA BRAISED LAMB CHOPS

as a cook-and-serve dish   *serves 4*

In the days when oysters were cheap they were often added to meat dishes. Today they are an expensive luxury but soon this may change. Underneath that great Brighton Marina breakwater, huge tanks have been built to develop oyster beds and hatcheries for other marine produce. It is hoped in this way to bring the foods to a wide public. In this recipe the oysters have been added as an optional extra.

4 or more lamb chops, chump, loin or neck
1 tablespoon oil or cooking fat
2 onions, peeled and chopped
2 carrots, cleaned and sliced
1 pint (575 ml) water
¼ pint (150 ml) wine or cider (or extra water)

1 chicken stock cube
½ teaspoon mixed herbs or thyme
salt and pepper
potatoes (optional)
1 level tablespoon homemade roux (p. 14) or packet soup-mix
8 or more oysters (optional)

1 Remove skin and some fat from chops.
2 Put oil or fat into Cooker and turn to 340 (4).
3 When light goes out, fry chops on both sides until browned.
4 Add onions and fry for 2 minutes, then add carrots, liquid, crumbled stock cube, herbs and seasoning.
5 Reduce heat to Simmer and cover with Cooker lid. Close vent.
6 Cook for 1–1½ hours, depending upon type of chops. They should be very tender. Add more water if necessary.
7 Whole potatoes may be added to the gravy about 15 minutes after cooking begins.
8 When cooked, thicken gravy with homemade roux or packet soup-mix.
9 Lastly add the oysters, if used, and heat through for only 2 minutes.

LAMB CHOP CASSEROLE

This recipe is similar to the Brighton Marina Braised Lamb Chops (*p. 87*). It has two differences. The chops are cooked in a casserole dish inside the Cooker, and the oysters have been omitted (though you could add them if you wished).

1 Halve the quantity of ingredients suggested on p. 87, but reduce water to ¼ pint (150 ml).
2 Put casserole dish into Cooker and turn heat to 420 (6). A metal or enamel dish will fry more quickly.
3 Put fat into dish and, when sizzling, fry trimmed chops until lightly browned on both sides. Remove chops to a plate. Add onions and fry for 2 minutes, then stir in 1 level tablespoon flour.
4 Add liquid and the other ingredients. Put chops back. When gravy begins to bubble, reduce heat to 300 (3), put on casserole lid and Cooker lid. Close vent. Cook for about 1¼–1½ hours, or until chops are very tender.

Jacket potatoes may be cooked around the dish. See Note, p. 69.

Mint flavoured: Add 2 or 3 teaspoons mint jelly with the liquid.

Spanish style: Add 2 sliced, canned red pimentos and use half water and half pimento juice for the liquid. Flavour with 2 teaspoons Worcester sauce, 1 crushed clove of garlic (or 1 teaspoon garlic salt or powder) and 2 teaspoons brown sugar.

Curried lamb chop casserole: Add curry powder to taste, about 3–5 heaped teaspoons. Add a little tart jam, 2 tablespoons sultanas or raisins, 2 heaped teaspoons brown sugar, 1 peeled chopped sweet apple and 1 tablespoon desiccated coconut. Fried mushrooms may be used as a garnish.

BAKED CRUMBED CHUMP CHOPS

as an oven

Chops of any sort should be cooked until completely tender and with this method, success is certain. Potatoes, dry pumpkin or sweet potatoes (kumaras) may be roasted at the same time.

1 or more chump chops per serving
potatoes or pumpkin or sweet
potatoes, or all three, cut into
pieces no more than 1 in
(3·5 cm) thick (optional)
1 or more tablespoons oil or other

cooking fat, depending on
number of chops
salt
milk
dry breadcrumbs or wheatgerm
gravy (p. 190)

1 Remove skin from edges of chops to prevent curling (unless the butcher has already done so). Wash and dry with kitchen paper.
2 If using potatoes put them into boiling, salted water for a few minutes then drain well.
3 Put fat into Cooker and turn heat to 380 (5).
4 Add a little salt to the milk. Dip chops first into that then into the crumbs or wheatgerm.
5 Put chops and vegetables in the hot fat and fry for 5 minutes on one side. Turn over. Cover with Cooker lid and close vent.
6 Reduce heat to 300 (3) and bake for about 45 minutes or until tender. Turn over about half way through the cooking, and open vent. If baking too fast, lower heat. When cooked, lift out with vegetables and make gravy.

PAN-FRIED LOIN CHOPS

1 Put 1 or 2 tablespoons oil or fat into Cooker and turn heat to 340 (4).
2 Trim a little of the fat from the edges of the chops and snip here and there to prevent curling. Dust lightly with flour and sprinkle with salt and pepper.
3 When fat is hot, fry the chops for a few minutes on each side to brown, then lower heat and fry until tender, about another 20 minutes. Turn during frying.

STUFFED LAMB CHUMP CHOPS

The stuffing not only adds flavour and interest, but enlarges the chops to make each more satisfying.

Stuffing (see below)
*4 chump chops cut 1¼ in (3 cm)
  thick, with a pocket cut by the
  butcher*
flour

*salt and pepper
2 tablespoons fat or 3 tablespoons
  oil
potatoes*

1 Make stuffing. Trim edges of chops and fill cavities. Secure with tiny skewers or thread. Dust all over with flour and sprinkle with salt and pepper.
2 Put fat into Cooker and turn heat to 380 (5).
3 Peel potatoes and put into boiling, salted water for 3 minutes.
4 When fat is very hot, put in chops and fry for 5 minutes.
5 Drain potatoes and put into the fat. Turn over to coat with the fat. See Note for sautéd potatoes.
6 Turn chops over and reduce heat to 300 (3). Cover with Cooker lid and open vent.
7 Let the fat sizzle, but not too violently. If cooking too quickly, lower heat.
8 Cook for 50–60 minutes, basting twice. Turn again if necessary.
9 When cooked, lift out with potatoes and keep hot. Spoon out all but 1 tablespoon of the fat and make gravy (*p. 190*).

Note: If you would rather sauté the potatoes, cut into ¼ in (0·5 cm) slices. Drop into the boiling, salted water for 2 minutes, drain well, dry and put into the fat for the last 30 minutes. Turn over during cooking to brown evenly.

Stuffing: For 4 chops, allow 8 tablespoons fresh breadcrumbs, 1 small grated onion, 1 tablespoon chopped parsley, ½ teaspoon thyme, salt and pepper and 2 tablespoons water. Mix well.

MOUSSAKA

A traditional Greek meat dish. Aubergines (also called egg plant) are the important ingredient but if they are unavailable or not popular with the family, say nothing (to the Greeks) and use peeled, sliced cucumber instead. I have tried it and it makes a delicious moussaka.

about 8 oz (225 g) aubergine or cucumber (see above)
1 tablespoon oil or butter
1 medium-sized onion, peeled and finely chopped
¾–1 lb (350–450 g) cooked lamb, minced (or beef, veal or pork would do)
1 well-crushed clove of garlic, or use garlic salt or powder

salt and pepper
½ lb (225 g) tomatoes, peeled and sliced
1 teaspoon sugar
¼ pint (150 ml) Cheese Sauce (p. 189)
grated cheese and dry breadcrumbs for topping

1 Cut the aubergine into ⅛ in (0·3 cm) slices and drop into a bowl of cold water, adding 1 level teaspoon salt. Allow to soak for 30 minutes or longer. No need to soak cucumber.

2 Heat fat in a small pan and fry onion for 2 minutes. Add meat and garlic and fry for another 2 minutes. Season with salt and pepper.

3 Put rack in Cooker and turn heat to 420 (6).

4 Use a 6–6½ in (16 cm) dish about 3 in (7·5 cm) deep.

5 Tip aubergines into a strainer and run fresh cold water through, to remove salt and aubergine juices. Put half into the dish. Cover with half the tomatoes. Sprinkle with salt and pepper and ½ teaspoon sugar.

6 Put in half the meat then the rest of the aubergines. Cover with the rest of the meat then the rest of the tomatoes. Sprinkle again with salt, pepper and ½ teaspoon sugar.

7 Pour over the cheese sauce and top with the grated cheese and breadcrumbs. Place on rack, cover with Cooker lid and open vent. Cook for 35 minutes.

ROAST PORK

To produce crisp, crackly crackling, fierce initial heat is needed. Thi
shocks the crackling into becoming porous and short—just the righ
texture for those crunchy bites. Adding a little sugar to the fat at th
beginning helps to brown the gravy.

3 tablespoons lard or dripping	potatoes, peeled, for roasting
leg or loin of pork, any suitable size	1 teaspoon sugar
	gravy (p. 190)
oil	apple sauce, or pineapple or
salt and pepper	orange slices

1 Put fat into Cooker and turn to 420 (6).
2 Have pork rind scored finely. Rub in oil and some salt.
3 Put potatoes into boiling, salted water for 5 minutes.
4 When fat is very hot, put in the pork, rind side down. Cool
   briskly for about 5 minutes until crisp. Sprinkle sugar into fat.
5 Turn meat over and reduce heat to about 300 (3), or gentl
   sizzling. Reduce heat again if necessary.
6 Put drained potatoes into the fat and turn over to coat wel
   Sprinkle with salt and pepper.
7 Cover with Cooker lid and open vent. After 30 minutes, tur
   potatoes and baste meat. Repeat twice more.
8 Allow 35 minutes per lb (½ kg) and 35 minutes extra, or longer. I
   crackling has softened towards the end, raise heat a little and tur
   meat over to crisp in the fat. Make gravy and serve with the sauc
   or fruit.

Roast pork with sage and onion stuffing: Make stuffing b
mixing 4 oz (100 g), or 2 cups, fresh breadcrumbs; 1 medium-size
onion, finely chopped; 1 teaspoon sage; 1 tablespoon choppe
parsley; 1 teaspoon salt and a little pepper; and 3 teaspoons butte
or margarine, chopped in roughly. Fill pocket (your butcher wi
cut this for you) with stuffing and secure with cocktail sticks o
thread.

PORK-AND-BEANS WITH GREEN HARICOTS
(Flageolets Verts)

serves 4

'ork-and-beans has a familiar sound and the two certainly marry
'ell. This recipe contains the canned green haricot beans with their
istinctive flavour; the following recipe has the more traditional
avour and appearance. The former is time-saving but more
xpensive; the latter cheaper but more trouble.

teaspoon butter or margarine	a 9½ oz (262 g) can of flageolets
pork spare rib chops or other	verts
pork slices	wine, cider or water
large onion, peeled and chopped	1 bay leaf
level dessertspoon flour	salt and pepper
large or 2 smaller carrots,	1 crushed clove of garlic, or 1
cleaned and sliced	teaspoon garlic salt or powder
	(optional)

Put casserole into Cooker and turn heat to 420 (6). Metal dishes
are better for frying quickly but other types would do. Put in the
fat.

Trim the pork and cut in halves. Add to fat and allow to sear while
the rest of the ingredients are being prepared. Move about and
turn to brown evenly. Take out pork and put on a plate.

Add onions to casserole and cook for 3 minutes, then stir in the
flour and mix with the onions. Add carrots.

Open can of beans and strain, saving the liquid. Put liquid into a
measuring jug and make up to ½ pint (275 ml) with wine, cider or
water. Add liquid to casserole. Stir to mix well.

Add bay leaf, then seasoning and garlic, if used. Put meat back.
Do not add beans yet.

Wait until gravy begins to boil, then cover with casserole lid and
Cooker lid. Close vent. Reduce heat to 300 (3) or a gentle boil and
allow about 1¾ hours. Reduce heat further if necessary. When
cooked, stir in the flageolets.

'ote: If there are more flageolets in the can than you feel you need in
ae casserole, save some to serve with fish (*see p. 35*).

PORK-AND-BEANS WITH TOMATO

In this recipe the beans are not tipped from a can but are soaked for several hours, then cooked to tenderness with the meat and toma If this seems a chore, see Note.

3 oz (75 g) small dried haricot
* beans*
¼ pint (275 ml) hot water
1 teaspoon margarine
3 pork belly slices, about 1 lb
* (½ kg)*
1 large onion, peeled and chopped
1 level tablespoon packet
* tomato soup-mix*

3 tomatoes, peeled and sliced
1 level dessertspoon brown sugar
2 teaspoons Worcester sauce
½ teaspoon seasoning salt
salt and pepper
1 crushed clove of garlic, or 1
* teaspoon garlic salt or powder*
* (optional)*

1 Put beans and water into a bowl and allow to soak for several hou or overnight, or to hasten this pour 2 pints (1 litre) water i Cooker and stand bowl in it. Turn heat to just below Simmer a keep water hot (but not boiling). The beans will be sufficien soaked in 1½ hours.

2 Remove bowl of beans and tip away the water in the Cooker.

3 Put casserole dish in Cooker and turn heat to 420 (6). Add marg ine to dish and allow to melt.

4 Trim edges and some fat from pork and add to dish. Allow to se while the other ingredients are being prepared.

5 When meat has seared on both sides, remove and put on a pla

6 Add onions to casserole and cook for 3 minutes. Add soup mix a mix in. Cook for another 2 minutes.

7 Add beans with liquid, tomatoes, sugar, Worcester sauce a seasoning. Garlic may be added if liked.

8 Stir, then put the meat back. Wait until gravy begins to boil, th cover with casserole lid and Cooker lid. Close vent. Reduce h to 300 (3) and boil gently for 2 hours. Lower heat further if boili too quickly.

Note: Canned haricot beans, butter beans or kidney beans m replace the dried haricot beans.

PORK WITH PINEAPPLE

as a cook-and-serve dish   *serves 4*

This is a pork recipe with a difference. The meat is first browned in
the Cooker, then lifted on to the rack and cooked above a tasty gravy.
The topping of pineapple rings helps to keep the meat moist.

*4 pork chops, spare ribs or belly
    slices, about ¾ in (2 cm) thick*
2 tablespoons oil or fat
*about 6 oz (175 g) onion, peeled
    and chopped*
*1 lb (½ kg) can of pineapple rings,
    and the pineapple syrup made
    up to 1 pint (575 ml) with hot
    water*

*¼ pint (150 ml) white wine or
    cider*
1 tablespoon soy sauce
1 teaspoon French mustard
½ teaspoon sage
salt and pepper if needed
stuffed olives

1 Trim some of the fat from the meat.

2 Put oil or fat into Cooker and turn to 340 (4).

3 When light goes out, fry pork on both sides until browned. Lift
    out and put on a plate.

4 Spoon off surplus fat and add onions. Fry until lightly browned,
    then reduce heat down to Simmer.

5 Add pineapple syrup with water and wine or cider (much of this
    liquid will boil down), soy sauce, mustard, sage and, if necessary,
    a little seasoning to taste.

6 Spoon a little liquid over the meat, then put a low rack in Cooker
    and place meat on it. Cover with Cooker lid and close vent.
    Simmer for 45 minutes.

7 Open up and turn meat over. Put a pineapple ring on top of each
    piece. Add more water, depending on how much has boiled off.
    Cover again and continue cooking for 30–40 minutes, or until pork
    is tender.

8 Lift on to a serving dish and top with sliced stuffed olives. The
    gravy may be thickened with ½–1 tablespoon of either homemade
    roux (*p. 14*) or packet soup-mix.

Note: Peeled potatoes may be placed on the rack with the meat.

Tried. neat to doe.

SAUTÉD PORK CHOPS WITH APPLE RINGS AND TOMATOES

as a frypan

Ask your butcher for thinly cut pork chops (some supermarkets se
them in packets). These fry in a short time. They are excellent for
quick after-office meal. Extras could include some commerci
'cook-in-sauce' and frozen French fried potatoes ready to rehea

pork chops, cut thin (about ¼ in
(0·5 cm))
salt and pepper
1 or 2 tablespoons oil
or other fat (quantity
depending on number of chops)
eating apples, unpeeled, cored and
sliced into ⅜ in (0·75 cm) rings,
½–1 apple per chop

tomatoes, peeled and halved, 1–
per chop
sugar
a few tablespoons commercial
'cook-in-sauce' (optional)
mushrooms, washed and sliced
(optional)
frozen French fried potatoes
(optional)

1 Snip edges of chops to prevent curling. Trim if you like less fa
   Sprinkle with salt and pepper.
2 Put oil or fat into Cooker and turn to 340 (4).
3 When very hot, put in the chops and fry on one side for about
   minutes. Turn over and continue frying. Reduce heat to 300 (3)
   gentle frying. They will need about 15 minutes. Thicker chop
   ½–¾ in (1·5 cm) thick, will need about 40 minutes slow fryin
4 Add the apples about 10 minutes before chops will be cooked. F
   them for about 4–5 minutes on each side. Add the tomatoes
   minutes after the apples. Sprinkle them with salt and pepper and
   little sugar. Mushrooms could be cooking as well.
5 If you decide on the sauce, it could be heating in a small containe
   (a freezer foil dish) in one corner of the Cooker. The French frie
   potatoes could be cooked either before or after the chops (unle
   there is room during the cooking).

PORK LAYERED HOT-POT

as an oven
serves 3–4

A simple but delicious combination of flavours accompanies the pork—onions, apples, tomatoes and herbs. Everything is cooked in a casserole dish sitting in the Cooker.

2 teaspoons of margarine or 3 teaspoons of oil	4 tomatoes, skinned and sliced
3 or 4 pork chops, fillets or spare ribs	1 level teaspoon dried basil
2 medium-sized onions, peeled and chopped	4 teaspoons sugar
3 heaped teaspoons flour	salt and pepper
2 medium-sized eating apples, peeled and sliced	1 bay leaf broken into 2 pieces
	1 chicken stock cube
	6 tablespoons water or wine

1 Put casserole dish into cold Cooker and add the fat or oil. Turn heat to 420 (6). Let fat get very hot.
2 Meanwhile, trim the pork.
3 Fry the pork in the hot fat on both sides for a few moments, then lift them out on to a plate.
4 Mix the onions with the flour and put half into the casserole dish. Cover with half the sliced apples, then with 2 of the tomatoes. Add half the basil.
5 Sprinkle with half the sugar and with salt and pepper. Arrange the pork on top.
6 Repeat with another layer of floured onions, apples and tomatoes and again sprinkle with sugar, salt and pepper and the rest of the basil. Add bay leaf.
7 Add stock cube to liquid and pour in.
8 When gravy begins to boil, cover with casserole lid and Cooker lid. Close vent. Reduce heat to 300 (3) or 260 (2) and allow to simmer for $1\frac{1}{4}$–$1\frac{1}{2}$ hours. Remove bay-leaf pieces before serving.

Note: Mushrooms, carrots or other vegetables can be added. A sprinkling of monosodium glutamate always heightens the flavours.

PORK WITH APPLE AND CIDER

as a cook-and-serve dish *serves 4*

Pork chops, spare ribs or fillets are cooked directly in the Cooker and may be served from it at the table. The combination of flavours makes a heavenly gravy.

4 or more pork chops, spare ribs or fillets
1 tablespoon cooking fat or 1½ tablespoons of oil
1 large or 2 smaller onions, peeled and chopped, or use frozen chopped onions
½ pint (275 ml) hot water
½ pint (275 ml) cider

1 large eating apple, peeled and sliced
3 sticks of celery, or 2 of leeks (or both), trimmed and sliced
1 bay leaf
1 tablespoon homemade roux (p. 14) or 2 level tablespoons packet soup-mix (celery or asparagus)
salt and pepper

1 Trim chops or spare ribs. Fillets are rather lean.
2 Put fat or oil into Cooker and set heat at 340 (4).
3 When fat is very hot, fry meat until lightly browned on one side. Add onions and cook while the meat is browning on the other side. Add water, cider, apple, vegetables and bay leaf.
4 Reduce heat to 220 (1) or quietly boiling. Cover with lid and close vent. Reduce heat if boiling too fast.
5 Simmer for about 1½ hours or until tender. Add more water if necessary.
6 Lastly, thicken with the roux or soup mix and continue cooking for 5 minutes. Taste and season with salt and pepper.

Casserole method: Use the same ingredients, but reduce both cider and water to ¼ pint (150 ml) each, or use all cider. Put casserole into Cooker and turn heat to 420 (6). Put in the fat and when hot fry chops and remove to a plate. Instead of the roux, use 1 level tablespoon flour, or the soup mix. Add this to the onions, in the pan, then add the liquid and all the other ingredients. Put the chops back. Cover with casserole lid and Cooker lid and close vent. Allow about 1½ hours.

GAMMON DOUBLE-DECKER IN A PARCEL

as an oven   serves 2

Many stores sell slices of gammon in packets, either singly or in pairs. Alternatively a butcher will cut it for you. Powdered bay leaf is available in jars and is handy for many savoury dishes. With jacket potatoes and another vegetable, a whole course can be cooked at the same time.

2 slices of gammon, about ¼ in (0·5 cm) thick and each weighing about 8 oz (225 g)
¼ medium-sized onion, peeled and grated or finely chopped
the same quantity of apple, finely chopped (or use chopped pineapple)

jacket potatoes, small-to-medium-sized (optional)
a sprinkling of bay-leaf powder or 1 bay leaf, halved
1 rounded teaspoon sugar
an extra vegetable (optional)
a sauce (optional)

1 Cut rind from gammon and, if salty, soak in hot water for about 20 minutes. With sugar-cured gammon, this is not necessary. Scrub potatoes, if used.

2 Put rack into Cooker and turn heat to 420 (6).

3 Cut a piece of foil about 11 in by 16 in (27·5 cm by 40 cm). Rinse gammon and place one slice sideways on the centre of the foil. Pile on the onion and sprinkle with bay-leaf powder or bay-leaf halves. Cover with the apple (or pineapple) and sprinkle with the sugar. Put the other slice of gammon on top. Lift up the sides of the foil over the edge of the gammon. Lift up ends and fold together to make a parcel. Seal well. Place on rack. Arrange the potatoes around.

4 Cover with Cooker lid and close vent. Leave at 420 (6) for 30 minutes then lower heat to 380 (5). Another vegetable may then be put into a smaller covered container, with hot water and salt, and cooked on the rack. Allow another 30 minutes with vent open.

5 Meanwhile make a sauce, if liked; Cheese Sauce (p. 189) for instance.

6 When gammon is cooked, lift out parcel, open carefully and stir juice into sauce.

ROAST VEAL WITH BACON AND MUSHROOM STUFFING

as an oven

If this is for a special occasion, Toast Baskets (*p. 62*) filled with cooked peas would make an attractive garnish.

3 tablespoons oil or fat
fillet end of leg of veal, any
    suitable size, with a pocket for
    stuffing
potatoes, peeled, for roasting
1 teaspoon sugar
gravy (p. 190)
Toast Baskets (p. 62)
    (*optional:* see above)

STUFFING
1 rasher of streaky bacon, rind
    removed and cut into ½ in
    (1·25 cm) pieces
2 oz (50 g) mushrooms, washed
    and sliced
1 small onion, peeled and grated
3 oz (75 g), or 1½ cups, fresh
    breadcrumbs
¼ teaspoon thyme
salt and pepper
3 teaspoons butter or margarine

1. Make stuffing: put bacon in Cooker and turn to 300 (3). Fry for 2 minutes, then add mushrooms and onion. When cooked, lift out and put into a bowl. Add breadcrumbs, thyme, salt and pepper. Roughly chop in the butter or margarine.

2. Add fat to Cooker and heat to 380 (5). Put stuffing into cavity and secure with thread or cocktail sticks. Brown meat on one side in the hot fat.

3. Meanwhile, put potatoes in boiling, salted water for 5 minutes.

4. Lift out meat and place a 6½ in (16 cm) rack or piece of foil in Cooker (the rack should be upside down so as to almost touch base). Put meat on this, browned side up. Drain potatoes, arrange round meat on the floor of the Cooker and turn to coat with the fat. Sprinkle sugar into the fat. Cover with Cooker lid and open vent. Reduce heat to 300 (3).

5. After 30 minutes turn potatoes and baste meat. Continue cooking, turning potatoes and basting once or twice more.

6. Allow 35 minutes per lb (½ kg) and an extra 35 minutes, or longer if necessary. Make gravy.

ESCALOPES DE VEAU

Perfect for a relaxed, romantic evening. If you have the veal marinating well beforehand, the mushrooms washed, one can of asparagus tips and another of tiny new potatoes ready to be opened, the main course will be on the table in no time.

2 escalopes of veal, each weighing about 4 oz (100 g) and beaten to ⅛ in (0·3 cm) thickness by the butcher
juice of 1 small lemon
1 good tablespoon butter
6 oz (175 g) mushrooms, washed and sliced
flour

4 tablespoons white wine with 2 tablespoons water, or 2 tablespoons Italian vermouth with 4 tablespoons water
2 tablespoons single cream
salt and pepper
garlic, if desired (see Note)
chopped parsley

1 Put veal on a shallow plate and pour on the lemon juice. Allow to marinate for an hour or longer, turning once or twice.

2 Put butter in Cooker and turn to 340 (4). Heat, but do not brown.

3 Put mushrooms at one end of Cooker and begin to fry.

4 Snip edges of veal to prevent curling, then shake free of juice and dust sparingly with flour. Fry in Cooker for 2 minutes on each side.

5 Lower heat to 300 (3) and lift out mushrooms. Keep them warm on a plate (under the Cooker would do).

6 Continue to cook the veal for about 5 minutes on each side, or longer if the meat is thicker. Lift on to a serving dish and keep warm.

7 Put mushrooms back into Cooker and add wine, water, cream, and salt and pepper to taste. Stir together and when hot pour over the escalopes. Sprinkle with chopped parsley.

Note: A garlic flavour may be given in several ways. Before heating, the Cooker could be rubbed with a cut clove of garlic; or garlic salt or powder could be sprinkled on the veal when it is floured. If it's a romantic evening, be sparing with the garlic.

Escalopes de veau with apricots and apricot brandy: Replace wine with 2 tablespoons of apricot brandy and 2 of apricot syrup. Heat canned or cooked dried apricots and use to garnish the veal.

Escalopes de veau with bacon, mushrooms and tomatoes: Reduce butter to 1 level dessertspoon and before adding mushrooms, fry 2 rashers of bacon cut into 1 in (2·5 cm) pieces. When the fat runs out, put mushrooms in at one end of the Cooker with tomato slices and push the bacon there too. Fry the meat in the bacon fat and butter. Add both bacon and mushrooms to the sauce. Garnish with tomatoes.

Escalopes de veau with pineapple and sweetcorn: While frying mushrooms, fry also pineapple slices. Lift both out until needed. Serve the veal garnished with the pineapple and heated cream-style sweetcorn. This could replace the sauce.

Wiener Schnitzel: The escalopes need to be even thinner for this. Ask a knowledgeable butcher for the right thickness. After taking them from the lemon juice, dust with flour, then coat first with beaten egg mixed with 1 tablespoon water, then with fine dry breadcrumbs or wheatgerm. Fry in the hot butter for 2 minutes on each side. If not tender, fry for a few minutes longer.

VEAL CASSEROLE WITH CORN

as an oven or as a cook-and-serve dish   *serves 2–3*

A larger quantity may be cooked in a larger casserole, or directly in the Cooker and taken to the table for serving: see Note.

½ lb (225 g) stewing or pie veal
¼ lb (100 g) streaky bacon
1 level tablespoon flour
1 medium-sized onion,
   peeled and chopped, or use
   frozen chopped onions
3 tablespoons sweetcorn kernels
   and juice

1 tablespoon lemon juice with 1
   teaspoon sugar or 2 tablespoons
   sherry or wine
6 tablespoons water
salt and pepper
1 bay leaf
1 or 2 sticks of celery, chopped

1 Put casserole dish into Cooker and set heat at 420 (6).

2 Trim veal. Cut veal and bacon into 1½ in (3·75 cm) pieces and when light goes out, drop both into casserole dish. Fry together for a few minutes, then add onion and fry for another 2 minutes. Stir in the flour and cook for a further minute.

3 Then add sweetcorn, lemon juice or sherry or wine, then water. Stir well and add seasoning.

4 Add bay leaf. When gravy begins to boil, reduce heat to 300 (3) or simmering. Cover with casserole lid then Cooker lid and close vent.

5 Allow 1½ hours. After 45 minutes add the celery. When cooking time is up, taste and add more seasoning if necessary.

Note: To cook in the pan—follow above recipe, but make the following changes. Fry everything in the Cooker except the flour. Add an extra ¾ pint (425 ml) hot water (much of this will boil off). Simmer at a low temperature, making sure the water is not boiling away too quickly. At the end thicken with 1 tablespoon of homemade roux (*p. 14*) or 1 rounded tablespoon packet soup-mix, any pale-coloured variety.

With asparagus: Replace the water with asparagus liquid from cooked or canned asparagus. Cut off the stalks (put aside any tough ones) and add to the veal about 10 minutes before cooking time is up. Garnish the dish with the tips.

BLANQUETTE OF VEAL

as an oven   *serves 4*

Blanquette means a white meat in a white gravy, and veal can claim the original and legitimate title. The Chicken Blanquette on p. 112 is therefore a plagiary. Whether for 1 serving or 6, or more, the casserole method seems to be the most satisfactory for this dish.

1 tablespoon oil or other fat
1¼–1½ lb (625–775 g) stewing veal
1 Spanish onion, peeled and chopped, or use frozen, chopped onions
1, or more, well-crushed cloves of garlic, or use garlic salt or powder (optional)
1 level tablespoon flour or 1 rounded tablespoon of packet soup-mix

1 large cup of chopped celery or a mixture of vegetables, or frozen stew-pack
¼ pint (150 ml) water or white wine
½ large or 1 small pale chicken stock cube
1 bay leaf
6 tablespoons single cream or evaporated milk
1 small can of creamed mushrooms
salt and pepper

1 Put casserole dish into cold Cooker and set heat at 420 (6). Add oil or fat and allow to get hot.
2 Trim veal and cut into 1½ in (3·75 cm) pieces. Add to casserole dish with onion. Add garlic if liked. Fry for a few minutes without allowing meat or onion to colour.
3 Sprinkle either flour or soup mix into dish and stir until onions and meat are coated.
4 Add the other vegetables, then the liquid, crumbled stock cube and bay leaf.
5 When gravy begins to simmer, put on casserole lid then cover with Cooker lid and close vent. Reduce heat to 300 (3).
6 After 30 minutes open up and look. If gravy is boiling too fast reduce heat to 220 (1). Continue cooking allowing 1 hour more.
7 Lastly, add cream or evaporated milk and creamed mushrooms. Season with salt and pepper. Remove bay leaf.

Jacket potatoes may be cooked around the dish. See Note, p. 69.

ROAST CHICKEN WITH A STUFFING

as an oven

Modern methods of chicken-rearing mean that at least the birds are more tender than they used to be and so take less time to cook. A 'free range' chicken (though more flavoursome) may toughen its muscles with exercise, whereas its battery cousin just sits and eats— and no doubt wonders what on earth it was hatched for!

1 chicken
potatoes, peeled, for roasting
4 tablespoons oil or other fat
3–4 rashers of streaky bacon
salt and pepper
1 teaspoon sugar

STUFFING
4 oz (100 g), or 2 cups, fresh
* breadcrumbs*
1 small onion, peeled and grated
* or finely chopped*
1 tablespoon walnuts, chopped
1 tablespoon dates, chopped
1 dessertspoon chopped parsley
½ teaspoon thyme
½ teaspoon salt and a little pepper
3 teaspoons butter or margarine

1 Thaw bird thoroughly if frozen. Remove bag of giblets and boil in 1 pint (575 ml) water to use for gravy.

2 Mix ingredients for the stuffing, adding the butter or margarine last, chopped in roughly. Spoon into rear cavity of chicken and secure with thread or a small skewer. Tie legs together.

3 Put potatoes into boiling, salted water for 5 minutes.

4 Put fat into Cooker and turn heat to 380 (5). When very hot, brown the bird on each side. Lift out.

5 Place a 6½ in (16 cm) low rack or piece of foil in Cooker. Put bird on it. Baste with the fat and cover the breast with bacon rashers. Put in potatoes and turn to coat with fat. Sprinkle with salt and pepper. Sprinkle sugar into fat; this will help to brown the gravy.

6 Cover with lid and open vent. Reduce heat to 300 (3) or less. The fat should sizzle gently. Allow 1–1½ hours or until bird is very tender. Turn potatoes and baste every 30 minutes.

7 When chicken is cooked, remove it to a warm serving dish with potatoes and keep hot while making gravy in Cooker using giblet stock for liquid.

STEAMED CHICKEN OR BOILING FOWL

as a large saucepan

Storage space may be saved in small kitchens by using the Cooker instead of a large saucepan. Of course if you have a pressure cooker as well, you have the best of both worlds.

A steamed chicken or boiling fowl may be used in many ways. The flavours steamed into it by the combination of ingredients provide delicious joints for picnics, and for cold salad platters.

2 pints (1¼ litres) water, or part vegetable water
1 medium-sized onion, peeled and stuck with 4 cloves
1 or 2 carrots, cleaned
2 bay leaves

a few chopped celery tops or sticks, or 1 teaspoon celery salt
parsley stalks, if possible
salt and pepper
1 chicken or boiling fowl, or 2 small chickens

1 Pour water into Cooker and turn heat to 220 (1). Add all the flavouring ingredients.
2 Thaw chicken well if frozen. Remove giblets and rinse out inside. Wash giblets and put into the water.
3 Put rack into Cooker, and put chicken on it.
4 Cover with Cooker lid and close vent. Heat may be reduced a little if water is boiling too violently, but it should not go off the boil.
5 Allow 40–50 minutes for 2 small poussins or spring chickens, 1–1½ hours for a chicken, 2½–3 hours for a boiling fowl. Add more water if necessary and baste now and again.

Whole chicken served with a sauce and vegetables: An onion and caper sauce may be made by using half chicken broth and half milk and the onion that was cooked with the chicken. Remove the cloves, then chop and stir into sauce. Add capers.

CHICKEN EN DAUBE
(casserole)

as an oven *serves 2*

The word *daube* means a stew, but this is no ordinary one. The method is quick and simple and the final dish a classic. A larger casserole and extra ingredients all round will cope with more servings or larger appetites.

2 or more chicken joints, skinned and trimmed
1 medium-sized onion, peeled and chopped or use 2 tablespoons frozen chopped onions
2–3 sticks of celery, cleaned and sliced
1 leek, trimmed and sliced
1 medium-sized carrot, cleaned and sliced
3 medium-sized tomatoes, skinned and sliced, or $\frac{1}{2}$ an 8 oz (225 g) can of peeled tomatoes with juice

1 teaspoon sugar
1 level dessertspoon packet soup-mix, any flavour
salt and pepper
potatoes (optional)

MARINADE
2 teaspoons soy sauce
3 tablespoons white wine or pale sherry
1 bay leaf and, if liked, 1 clove of garlic or a little garlic salt

1 Put chicken into a shallow bowl, and add the marinade ingredients. Turn once or twice while vegetables are being prepared (or leave for several hours or overnight).

2 Put a suitable-sized heatproof casserole into Cooker, and turn heat to 420 (6).

3 Put prepared vegetables into casserole. Add sugar and sprinkle in packet soup-mix. Mix well.

4 Arrange chicken on top and pour in the marinade liquid (removing clove of garlic if used). Add seasoning to taste.

5 Cover with casserole lid then with Cooker lid. Close vent. Allow to cook at the high heat until gravy begins to bubble, then turn down to 300 (3) and simmer for $1\frac{1}{2}$–2 hours, or until chicken is tender. Reduce heat if gravy is boiling too fast.

Jacket potatoes may be cooked around the dish. See Note, p. 69.

Long slow cooking: See method used for Chicken Casserole (3), p. 110. Begin at step 2.

HARICOT CHICKEN

Beans are more nourishing than potatoes, so if you wish, you can use them instead. If you decide to have both, jacket potatoes could be cooking at the same time on the floor of the Cooker. Increase amounts proportionally for more servings.

3 oz (75 g) small blackeye haricot
*   beans*
¼ pint (275 ml) hot water
1 onion, peeled and chopped
3 small or 2 larger tomatoes,
*   peeled and sliced*
salt and pepper and 1 teaspoon
*   sugar*

1 crushed clove of garlic, or a
*   little garlic salt or powder*
*   (optional)*
2 chicken portions
2 teaspoons flour
1 chicken stock cube
¼ teaspoon mixed herbs or thyme
other vegetables (optional)

1 Rinse beans and put into a bowl with the hot water. Allow to soak for about 6 hours or more, or overnight (*see Note*).

2 When beans are ready, put casserole dish into Cooker and turn heat to 420 (6).

3 Put beans into a strainer over a bowl and save the water. Tip beans into casserole. Cover with the onions, then the tomatoes and sprinkle with salt and pepper and the sugar. Add garlic if liked.

4 Skin and trim the chicken and dust with the flour. Place on top of the tomatoes. Sprinkle with salt and pepper.

5 Add crumbled cube and herbs to the water in which the beans were soaking and pour over chicken.

6 When gravy begins to bubble, reduce heat to 300 (3). Cover with casserole lid, then with Cooker lid and close vent. After 30 minutes, open up and look. If gravy is boiling too fast, lower heat to 220 (1). It should boil gently.

7 Allow about 1½–1¾ hours or until chicken is very tender.

Jacket potatoes may be cooked around the dish. See Note, p. 69.

Note: To save soaking, canned haricot beans may be used. Drain liquid away if it is very salty and use ¼ pint (150 ml) fresh water.

CHICKEN CASSEROLE (1)

as a cook-and-serve dish   serves 6

A dish for 4 or more people may be cooked in the Multi Cooker and taken directly to the table. But for 1 or 2, it is better to cook it in a casserole dish inside the Cooker. The recipe for this is given on the following page. See p. 110 for long slow cooking.

6 or more chicken joints
3 tablespoons oil or other cooking fat
2 large or 4 small onions, peeled and chopped, or use frozen chopped onions
¾ pint (425 ml) stock, or water with 2 chicken stock cubes; part white wine may be used

vegetables, such as chopped celery or carrots (see Note)
1 teaspoon thyme or rosemary
1, or more, crushed cloves of garlic, or 1 teaspoon garlic salt or powder (optional)
potatoes (optional)
2 level tablespoons packet soup-mix, any flavour
salt and pepper

1 Skin and trim the chicken.
2 Put oil or fat into Cooker and heat to 380 (5). When light goes out, fry chicken until lightly browned then remove and put on a plate.
3 Add onions and fry for 2 minutes, then turn down heat to 220 (1).
4 Add liquid, vegetables, thyme or rosemary and garlic, if liked.
5 Put the chicken back. Cover with Cooker lid and close vent. Reduce heat until gravy just simmers gently. Add more water from time to time if it is boiling away. Allow 1¼–1½ hours.
6 Whole peeled potatoes can be added after 30 minutes.
7 Ten minutes before cooking time is up, add packet soup-mix. Stir until thick, then taste and add seasoning.

Note: If you are short of time, there are very good frozen stew-packs of mixed vegetables on the market which will save much peeling and chopping.

CHICKEN CASSEROLE (2)

Small quantities need to be cooked in a smaller vessel sitting in the Cooker. This method may of course be used for larger quantities in a larger casserole.

1 level tablespoon oil or other fat
2 or more chicken joints
1 medium-sized onion, peeled and chopped, or use frozen chopped onions
1 level tablespoon flour
one or more other vegetables (see Note, p. 109)

¼ pint (150 ml) water or white wine, or half and half
½ chicken stock cube
½ teaspoon thyme or mixed herbs
salt and pepper
1 crushed clove of garlic, or a little garlic salt or powder (optional)

1 Put casserole dish in cold Cooker and turn heat to 420 (6). Put fat into casserole.
2 Skin and trim the chicken, and when fat is hot fry for a few minutes. Remove to a plate.
3 Add onions and fry for 2 minutes, then add flour and fry for another minute.
4 Add any other vegetables liked, then add liquid, crumbled stock cube, herbs, seasoning and garlic, if liked. Stir.
5 Put chicken back and spoon over the gravy.
6 When gravy just begins to simmer, reduce heat to 300 (3). Put on casserole lid then Cooker lid, and close vent. Allow 1¼–1½ hours, less for spring chicken or poussin, until chicken is tender and will come away from the bone. Reduce heat if gravy is boiling too fast.

Jacket potatoes may be cooked around the dish. See Note, p. 69.

Chicken casserole (3) (long slow cooking): Follow method for Chicken Casserole (2), but be sure to chop the onions and other vegetables very finely. When gravy begins to bubble (after step 5), lift out casserole and put in rack. Put casserole back, cover with lid then with Cooker lid, and close vent. Turn to 220 (1). Open up and look after 30 minutes and if the gravy is bubbling lower heat a little. Allow 6 hours.

CHICKEN BLANQUETTE WITH ASPARAGUS (1)
(casseroled)

as an oven   *serves 2*

The term *blanquette* is usually associated with veal, but as this is also a 'dish of white meat' the name may be applied. The tiny cocktail onions and the asparagus give the sauce an interesting and delicious flavour. It may be made in a casserole, as in this recipe, or directly in the Cooker; see the following page.

2 or more chicken joints, trimmed and skinned
1 level tablespoon flour or 1 rounded tablespoon packet soup-mix, any pale-coloured variety
6 oz (175 g) cooked or canned asparagus spears with ¼ pint (150 ml) liquid

8 white cocktail onions
2 sticks of celery, trimmed and chopped
3 tablespoons single cream
salt and pepper
chopped parsley

1 Place a heatproof casserole in Cooker and turn heat to 420 (6).
2 Coat chicken joints with the flour or, if using packet soup-mix, add the joints to casserole and sprinkle in soup mix.
3 Pour the asparagus liquid over the chicken. Add the cocktail onions and the celery. Mix in.
4 When gravy begins to simmer, reduce heat to 300 (3). Put on casserole lid and Cooker lid. Close vent. Cook for 1¼–1½ hours. About 15 minutes before chicken is ready, gently warm asparagus spears in a little butter in a small saucepan.
5 Finally, add the cream and seasoning. Sprinkle with chopped parsley and serve with the asparagus spears.

Jacket potatoes may be cooked around the dish. See Note, p. 69.

Long slow cooking: Use rack. At step 4 reduce heat to 220 (1). Allow 6 hours. Take a look after 1 hour, or less. The gravy should not be bubbling, but just moving gently. For longer cooking, 7–8 hours, reduce temperature to a little lower than 220 (1).

CHICKEN BLANQUETTE WITH ASPARAGUS (2)

as a cook-and-serve dish   *serves 4*

This is made in the Cooker and may be served directly from it. It is not suitable for less than 3 people. Smaller quantities should be cooked in a casserole sitting in the Cooker; see previous recipe.

2 tablespoons oil or margarine
4 or more chicken joints, trimmed and skinned
12 oz (350 g) cooked or canned asparagus spears with the asparagus liquid made up to 1¼ pints (750 ml) with hot water
16 white cocktail onions

4 sticks of celery, trimmed and chopped
2 rounded tablespoons homemade roux (p. 14) or packet soup-mix, any pale-coloured variety
5 tablespoons single cream
salt and pepper
chopped parsley

1 Put fat into Cooker and turn heat to 340 (4). When hot, fry chicken for a few minutes on either side without browning.
2 Add liquid and reduce heat to 220 (1). Add onions and celery.
3 Cover with Cooker lid and close vent. Cook for 1¼–1½ hours or until chicken is tender. Add more water if it boils down. By the end of cooking there should be about ¾ pint (425 ml). Reduce heat if boiling too fast. About 15 minutes before chicken is ready, gently warm asparagus spears in a little butter in a small saucepan.
4 Add roux or soup mix to chicken liquid. Both will dissolve readily. Cook for a few more minutes then turn off heat and add cream. Season with salt and pepper. Sprinkle with chopped parsley and serve with the asparagus spears.

Note: Peeled potatoes could be cooking in the gravy. Add 40–45 minutes before cooking time is up, depending on size of potatoes.

SAUTÉD CHICKEN PORTIONS

The secret of sautéing these pieces of chicken is to baste frequently with the fat. This way they will be moist as well as tender. Potatoes may be cooked at the same time.

2 tablespoons oil or other fat
2 chicken legs or other chicken
   portions
potatoes

salt
Mushroom Sauce (p. 189) or
   gravy (p. 190)

1 Put fat into Cooker and turn heat to 380 (5).
2 Trim chicken if necessary, but do not remove the skin. Rinse, and dry with kitchen paper. When fat is very hot, put in the chicken, skin side down, and fry until lightly browned, about 5 minutes.
3 Reduce heat to 300 (3) and turn chicken over. Baste well with the fat.
4 Potatoes may be halved and roasted, or cut into $\frac{1}{4}$ in (0·5 cm) slices and sautéd. In either case, pop them into salted, boiling water for 3 minutes first. Take out, drain and put into the fat. Turn over at once to coat with fat. Halved or whole potatoes should go in with the chicken, but the thin-sliced potatoes need only about 30 minutes.
5 Sauté chicken for about 1–1$\frac{1}{4}$ hours. Reduce heat if it is frying too fast and baste twice during the cooking. Turn potatoes half way through cooking to brown evenly.
6 Lift out chicken and potatoes on to serving dish and keep warm, spoon off all but 1 tablespoon of the fat and make either gravy or mushroom sauce.

Note: If making mushroom sauce, fry the washed, sliced mushrooms while the chicken is cooking, then add to the sauce. Alternatively, serve the mushrooms with the chicken then make gravy.

QUICK CHICKEN PILAF

The preparation of this dish takes very little time. Fling everything in together when you are ready, leave the kitchen and relax, and hey presto, dinner is served!

1 chicken breast (or 2 for special occasions)
¼ lb (225 g) natural wholegrain rice (a must for this dish)
2 pints (1 litre) water
1 chicken stock cube
1 large onion, peeled and chopped
¼ lb (225 g) carrots and 1 large parsnip, both scraped and sliced into rings
1 teaspoon dried tarragon or herb of your choice

1, or more, crushed cloves of garlic, or use garlic salt or powder (optional)
salt and pepper
1 medium-sized green pepper, seeds removed and sliced
1 cup cauliflower florets or peas
1 or more tablespoons chopped parsley

1 Cut chicken into small pieces.
2 Put rice and water into cold Cooker and turn heat to Simmer.
3 Add chicken, crumbled stock cube, onion, carrots, parsnip and herbs. Stir all together.
4 Add garlic, if liked, then seasoning.
5 Cover with Cooker lid and close vent.
6 Simmer gently for 40–45 minutes, or until rice is soft. Add more water if it is boiling away.
7 Lastly, add green pepper, cauliflower florets or peas (or both) and continue cooking for about 8 minutes.
8 Sprinkle with chopped parsley and serve from the dish.

Note: If you prefer to use the shorter-cooking, white long-grain rice, use ready-cooked chicken. Allow 15 minutes.

CHICKEN MARYLAND

as a deep fryer *serves 4*

If the chicken is to be crumbed it should be young enough to fry in about twenty minutes. If it is full-grown it should be cooked without a coating and for a longer time. See also Sautéd Chicken Portions (*p. 113*). These could be served with the same traditional Maryland accompaniments.

a 3 lb (1¼ kg) young spring chicken, jointed, or 4 chicken joints
1 tablespoon flour with 1 teaspoon salt and a little pepper

1¼ pints (725 ml) oil
1 egg
fine dry breadcrumbs or wheatgerm for coating

1 Trim chicken and remove skin.
2 Put flour and seasoning into a paper bag. Put in the joints two at a time and shake until well coated.
3 Put oil into Cooker and turn heat to 420 (6).
4 Beat the egg with 1 tablespoon water and pour on to a plate. Put breadcrumbs or wheatgerm on another plate.
5 Dip chicken joints first into the egg, then the coating.
6 Make sure that the oil is at the correct heat, 375°F (190°C). (Or, without a thermometer, test by dropping in a small cube of bread. If it sizzles fast and browns in 10 seconds the oil is ready.) Put the chicken in with tongs and fry for about 20 minutes, or until tender. Serve with Crumbed Bananas (*see below*) and Sweetcorn Fritters (*p. 50*) or canned cream-style sweetcorn.

Crumbed bananas: Unless bananas are very large and need cutting through horizontally, leave whole. Dip first in beaten egg, then in breadcrumbs and fry for a few minutes in the hot fat.

ROASTED GUINEA FOWL

as an oven   *serves 4–5*

This is one of the recipes in an early edition of Mrs Beeton's cookery book. Later editions were enlarged by others and so extended her original work. Thus changes were made to suit changing times. The guinea fowl in the nineteenth-century edition was to be 'roasted in front of a clear fire'; its average cost, four shillings.

1 guinea fowl
1 rasher of bacon
3 tablespoons oil or fat
½ teaspoon tarragon
1 pint (575 ml) water

ACCOMPANIMENTS
Sauce Espagnole (p. 189)
Buttered Breadcrumbs (see
    below)
Pommes Frites (p. 53)
watercress

1 Remove bag of giblets, wash the guinea fowl and tuck the bacon rasher into cavity. Secure opening with a tiny skewer or thread.
2 Put oil or fat into Cooker and set heat at 380 (5).
3 When light goes out, brown the bird on both breast and back.
4 Reduce heat to 300 (3). Cover with Cooker lid and open vent. Roast bird on its back for 30 minutes.
5 Meanwhile, boil the giblets with the tarragon in 1 pint (575 ml) water for about 20 minutes. This may be used to make sauce.
6 After 30 minutes, turn the bird so that its breast is in the fat. Roast there for another 30 minutes. If it is not sufficiently cooked, turn breast side up again and continue cooking a little longer.
7 Put on to a hot serving dish and make sauce espagnole. Serve with buttered breadcrumbs and pommes frites and garnish with watercress.

Buttered breadcrumbs: Melt 2 tablespoons butter in a saucepan and add 4 oz (100 g), or 2 cups, fresh breadcrumbs. Stir to coat well and crisp a little.

ROAST DUCK PORTIONS WITH APRICOTS

as an oven

Some supermarkets sell packaged duck portions but butchers usually prefer to sell the whole duck and joint it for you. In this recipe, the duck will bake to tenderness without drying. Potatoes may be roasted at the same time.

1 duck portion per serving, about 1 lb (½ kg)
2 tablespoons beef dripping or other fat
potatoes for roasting
salt and pepper

a 1 lb (450 g) can of apricot halves
1 level tablespoon flour
¼ pint (150 ml) each of water and apricot syrup
a few glacé or maraschino cherries for decoration

1 Rinse and wipe the duck.
2 Put fat into Cooker and turn heat to 340 (4).
3 When hot, put in the duck portions and baste immediately.
4 Peel the potatoes and cook in boiling, salted water for about 3 minutes. Lift out, drain and put into Cooker. Turn over to coat both sides with the fat. Sprinkle duck and potatoes with salt and pepper. Reduce heat to 300 (3).
5 Cover with Cooker lid and open vent.
6 Roast for about 1½–2 hours, turning both duck and potatoes twice and basting with fat each time.
7 For the last 30 minutes of roasting, turn Cooker lid slightly cornerwise to allow more steam to escape than the vent allows.
8 Strain syrup from apricots and warm apricots.
9 When duck is tender, lift out with potatoes and keep hot. Spoon off all but 1 tablespoon of the fat and add the flour. Cook for a few minutes, then add water and syrup. Cook until thick, adding salt and pepper.
10 Serve duck garnished with the apricots, each with a cherry in the centre. Serve sauce separately.

Note: A spicy flavour may be given to the sauce by adding about ½ teaspoon cinnamon and ¼ teaspoon nutmeg.

CHILLI CON RABBIT

With apologies to the South Americans for replacing their *carne* with the humble rabbit. Use a large casserole sitting in the Cooker.

4 rabbit legs or about 2½–3 lb
(1¼–1½ kg) jointed rabbit
1 level tablespoon flour
1 dessertspoon oil or other fat
2 rashers of streaky bacon, rinds
removed and cut into 1 in
(2·5 cm) pieces
1 medium-sized onion, peeled and
chopped

1 or 2 cloves of garlic, crushed
¼ pint (150 ml) water
10 oz (275 g) can of red kidney
beans
1 chicken stock cube
1 tablespoon chilli powder
1 level teaspoon oregano or
tarragon
salt and pepper

1 Put casserole (preferably metal or pottery) into Cooker and turn heat to 420 (6) or maximum.
2 Wash rabbit and dry on kitchen paper. Dust with all the flour.
3 Put oil or fat and bacon into casserole and cook until sizzling.
4 Add rabbit and fry for a few minutes, then lift out and put on a plate.
5 Add onions and well-crushed garlic cloves and fry for 2 minutes.
6 Add water and the liquid or sauce from the can of beans. (Reserve beans for later.) Add crumbled stock cube, chilli powder, herb and seasoning. Stir.
7 Put rabbit back in casserole and spoon over the gravy. When it begins to bubble, reduce heat to about 300 (3) or a gentle boil. Cover with casserole lid, then with Cooker lid and close vent.
8 Allow about 1¾–2 hours, or until rabbit is tender. If cooking too fast, reduce heat to 220 (1). Add the beans for the last 10 minutes.

Long slow cooking: Follow main recipe but be sure to chop the onions finely. At step 7, when gravy begins to bubble, lift casserole out and put in the rack. Put dish back, cover with casserole lid, then with Cooker lid and close vent. Reduce heat to 220 (1) or a gentle simmer. Look after the first 30 minutes and if gravy is bubbling, reduce heat to 220 (1). It should be just moving a little. Allow 6 hours. For 8 hours' cooking time reduce heat to between 220 (1) and Simmer.

RABBIT À L'ORANGE CASSEROLED

This recipe was really meant for duck, but there's no reason why the lowly but tasty rabbit shouldn't claim equal status—marinade and all. Double or treble the quantities for a supper party.

2 legs of rabbit, about 1 lb ($\frac{1}{2}$ kg)
1 tablespoon oil or other fat
2 level tablespoons flour
salt and pepper
1 orange
parsley

MARINADE
grated rind and juice of 1 orange
2 tablespoons Marsala or sherry
$\frac{1}{2}$ teaspoon ground coriander
$\frac{1}{2}$ teaspoon mixed herbs or 1 sachet of bouquet garni
1 teaspoon sugar
1 small onion, peeled and stuck with 3 cloves
1 clove of garlic, crushed (optional)

1 Mix all the ingredients for the marinade and put into a bowl.
2 Rinse rabbit and put into marinade. Leave for 4 or more hours, or overnight. Turn once or twice.
3 When ready to cook, put casserole dish into Cooker and turn to 420 (6). Add fat to dish and allow to melt. It will melt more quickly if the dish is metal or enamel.
4 Lift rabbit out of marinade, shake off excess liquid and dust with some of the flour. When fat is sizzling, fry rabbit until lightly browned then lift out and put on a plate.
5 Take onion from marinade and remove cloves. Chop and add to dish. Fry for a few minutes, adding the rest of the flour.
6 Add marinade liquid and season with salt and pepper. Mix well and then put rabbit back, spooning over the gravy.
7 When it begins to bubble cover with casserole lid, then Cooker lid. Close vent. Reduce heat to 300 (3). If boiling too fast reduce heat to 220 (1). Allow $1\frac{1}{2}$–2 hours.
8 Peel and slice the other orange and use as a garnish with sprigs of parsley.

Jacket potatoes may be cooked around the dish. See Note, p. 69.

PIGEONS WITH SPANISH SAUCE

An old way with pigeons, brought up to date.

2 pigeons
2 rashers of streaky bacon, rinds removed
1 tablespoon butter or margarine
1 onion, peeled and chopped
1 large or 2 small carrots, cleaned and sliced
1½ level tablespoons flour
¼ pint (150 ml) stock, or water with 1 chicken stock cube

1 tablespoon tomato purée
3 tablespoons claret or other red wine
1 teaspoon brown sugar
salt and pepper
1 or 2 crushed cloves of garlic, or use garlic salt or powder (optional)

1 Split pigeons down the middle and take out the sharp little breast bones, then cut off the meatless leg joints. These could be boiled for about 10 minutes in the water to make stock for the sauce.

2 Put a metal or enamel casserole dish into Cooker and set heat at 420 (6).

3 Cut bacon into 1½ in (3·75 cm) pieces and drop into casserole. Add butter or margarine. Fry bacon.

4 When fat has run out of bacon, fry the pigeons until lightly browned and lift them out on to a plate.

5 Add onions and carrots and fry for 3 minutes, then add flour. Cook for another 2 minutes.

6 Tip in the stock, or water and stock cube, tomato purée, claret, sugar and seasoning. Add garlic if liked. Stir well.

7 Put the pigeons back into the casserole. When gravy begins to simmer, cover with casserole lid, then with Cooker lid. Close vent. Reduce heat to 300 (3). Look after 30 minutes and if it is boiling too fast, reduce heat to 220 (1). Cook for 45–60 minutes.

As a cook-and-serve dish: The dish may be cooked in the pan and served from it. Fry pigeons in the pan at 340 (4), then continue with the recipe, but increasing water to 1 pint (575 ml). This will reduce during cooking. Leave thickening until the end and instead of flour use 1 tablespoon either homemade roux (*p. 14*) or packet soup-mix. Add more water if necessary.

Sausages

I once asked a butcher which type of sausage he would recommend: pork or beef. 'The public generally prefer pork,' he replied, 'but butchers mostly eat beef.' I have not done a survey of the preferences of butchers, so cannot verify the truth of the statement. Today an enticing array of different types of sausages is displayed: English or foreign, with or without skins, thin or fat, and with a variety of flavours and names. All will fry well in the Cooker.

If you prefer sausages without skins, either buy skinless or remove the skins thus: hold the sausage under a running cold tap, with a sharp knife slit it cleanly down the middle and, still under the tap, remove the skins.

TO FRY SAUSAGES

Put the sausages into a cold Cooker and set heat at 300 (3). If the pan is not non-stick and the surface is not smooth, add about 1–2 teaspoons butter, margarine or oil. Fry the sausages gently until browned, turning frequently. They should brown in 10–12 minutes. To hurry the frying, raise the heat to 320 (3½) or 340 (4), but be careful that they do not burn. If cooking fast they will need pricking here and there to prevent bursting.

Sausages with gravy: Lift out sausages and keep hot. If there have been many sausages and a lot of fat remains, spoon off all but about 1–2 tablespoons. For ¾ pint (425 ml) gravy, add 2 level tablespoons flour to the fat and cook at about 320 (3½) until beginning to brown. Stir in ¾ pint (425 ml) water and cook and stir until thick. Season with salt and pepper. If you are cooking vegetables to serve with the sausages, use some or all of the vegetable liquid instead of water, checking seasoning carefully.

Sausages with vegetables: Before frying the sausages, prepare the vegetables. Have 2 tomatoes for each serving: peel by putting them into boiling or very hot water for a few minutes, then slipping off the skin. Slice into 2 or 3 pieces. Finely chop 2 or more vegetables, such as onion, celery, carrot or leeks, or use frozen mixed vegetables—a stew-pack, for instance, consisting of onions, carrots, celery, turnip and swedes. Put a little butter, margarine or oil into the Cooker and bring heat to 300 (3). Add tomatoes and other vegetables and cook for 8–10 minutes. Push to one side, then add sausages. Cook both together until sausages have browned and the vegetables are cooked. Season with salt and pepper, and, if liked, 2 or 3 teaspoons of soy sauce.

Sausages with apple or pineapple rings: For apple rings, core sweet eating apples (they keep their shape better than cooking apples), and cut into $\frac{1}{2}$ in (1·25 cm) rings. An average apple will cut into four. Allow $1\frac{1}{2}$ tablespoons butter or margarine for 2–3 apples. Put fat into Cooker and set at about 340 (4). When fat is hot, put in the rings and fry for about 4 minutes on each side, or until browned. If not cooked, reduce heat and continue a little longer. If there is room, the sausages could be cooked at the same time. If not, put apples on a plate and sprinkle with sugar. Keep warm. Fry the sausages and serve with the rings.

For pineapple rings: if using canned pineapple drain the rings from syrup; for fresh pineapple, core then peel and cut into $\frac{1}{2}$ in (1·25 cm) rings. Fry as above and serve with the sausages.

Sausages with buckwheat: Fry the sausages. Allow 1 oz (25 g) toasted buckwheat and $\frac{1}{4}$ pint (150 ml) water per serving. When sausages have browned, spoon off excess fat, put in the buckwheat and add the water. Add also frozen or young fresh peas or beans, allowing about 3 oz (75 g) per serving. Season well with salt and pepper and, if you wish, 2 or 3 teaspoons soy sauce. This could replace some of the salt. Reduce heat to 220 (1) or a little lower and simmer for about 8 minutes, or until buckwheat has softened.

Other additions could be used, according to choice, such as skinned tomatoes; garlic cloves (well crushed) or garlic salt or powder; mushrooms, washed, sliced and fried with the sausages; sliced leeks or finely chopped onions.

Sausages with rice: Fry the sausages. Meanwhile, prepare additions. For instance, peeled and chopped onions; trimmed and chopped celery or leeks (or both); scraped and sliced carrots; washed, sliced mushrooms; peeled, sliced tomatoes or pimentos; or chopped peppers. Choose at least two additions. When sausages have browned, spoon off all but 1 tablespoon of the fat and add the rice. Allow 2–2½ tablespoons per person. Add water, allowing ¾ pint (425 ml) for 4 tablespoons rice. Reduce heat to simmering point, then put in any of the suggested additions. Season well with salt and pepper and allow about 15 minutes. Add more water if necessary. Add peppers towards the end of the cooking.

Note: If you wish to use natural wholegrain rice, pre-cook the rice separately for 25 minutes, drain well, then proceed with recipe, adding extra water if necessary.

Sausage ratatouille party bake: (Quantities are for 6 servings.) Prepare ingredients for Ratatouille (*p. 52*). Fry 2½ lb (1¼ kg) sausages. Put on a plate and keep hot. Tip away sausage fat and add 1 tablespoon oil, butter or margarine. When hot, add the ingredients for the ratatouille and fry for 20 minutes, stirring frequently. If wished cook rice separately while the ratatouille is cooking, allowing 1 lb (450 g) rice in 2 pints (1 litre) water. When ratatouille is ready arrange sausages on top and sprinkle with chopped parsley. Serve from the Cooker with the rice in a separate dish. Hot French bread is an alternative accompaniment. To heat, wrap in foil and warm in oven or under grill, turning once.

BRAISED KIDNEYS AND BACON (1)

as a cook-and-serve dish   *serves 4*

The kidneys will pan-cook well, provided the servings are for 4 or more, but a small amount for less than 4 is more satisfactory if cooked in a casserole sitting in the Cooker. See Braised Kidneys and Bacon (2) (*p. 125*).

8 or more lambs' kidneys, skinned
2 rashers of streaky bacon
1 large or 2 small onions, peeled and chopped, or use frozen chopped onions
1 pint (575 ml) hot water (or part water, part wine or sherry)
1 beef stock cube or 2 teaspoons soy sauce

½ teaspoon thyme or mixed herbs
1–2 well-crushed cloves of garlic, or 1–2 teaspoons garlic salt or powder (optional)
2 level tablespoons packet soup-mix, any flavour
salt and pepper (or replace salt with about 2 teaspoons soy sauce)

1 Prepare kidneys. Cut horizontally in halves and remove fatty cores. Cut each in half.
2 Remove rinds from bacon and cut rashers into 1½ in (3·75 cm) pieces. Drop into cold Cooker and set heat at 340 (4).
3 When bacon begins to sizzle add onions and kidneys. Fry for 4 minutes.
4 Reduce heat to 220 (1) and add liquid, stock cube or soy sauce, thyme or mixed herbs, and garlic, if used.
5 Stir together, then cover with Cooker lid and close vent. Simmer for 55 minutes. Add more water if gravy is reducing too much. By the end of cooking there should be about ¾ pint (425 ml).
6 Sprinkle in the soup mix. It will dissolve after a few minutes. Allow another 7 minutes. Season.

Braised ox kidney and bacon: Use 1 lb (450 g) ox kidney. Remove large core and tubes. Soak for about 15 minutes in warm water to remove strong flavour. Cut into small pieces then follow above recipe, allowing 1½–2 hours.

Braised veal kidneys: Use 2 complete veal kidneys. Treat as Braised Ox Kidney. Allow 20 minutes.

BRAISED KIDNEYS AND BACON (2)
(en casserole)

This casserole method is more suitable than Braised Kidneys and Bacon (1) (*p. 124*) for smaller quantities, but it is also excellent for large amounts and more servings.

4 or more lambs' or pigs' kidneys
1 rasher of bacon, cut into 1½ in (3·75 cm) pieces
1 onion, peeled and chopped, or use frozen chopped onions
1 level dessertspoon flour
¼ pint (150 ml) water (or wine or sherry)

1 beef stock cube
½ teaspoon thyme
salt and pepper (or replace salt with about 2 teaspoons soy sauce)
1–2 well-crushed cloves of garlic, or 1–2 teaspoons garlic salt or powder (optional)

1 Prepare kidneys as described in step 1, p. 124. Quarter the kidneys.
2 Put casserole dish into Cooker and set heat at 420 (6). When light goes out, put bacon into dish and fry.
3 Add onion and fry with the bacon for a few minutes. Toss kidneys in the flour and add. Fry everything together for 3 minutes.
4 Add water (or wine or sherry), stock cube, thyme, seasoning and garlic, if used. Stir everything together.
5 When gravy begins to simmer, reduce heat to about 300 (3). Put on casserole lid then cover with Cooker lid and close vent. Allow to simmer for 50–55 minutes. If after 15 minutes it is boiling too fast, lower to 260 (2).

Additions: Give a tomato flavour by adding 1 or 2 teaspoons tomato purée (or 2 peeled sliced tomatoes), 1 teaspoon sugar and 1 teaspoon Worcester sauce. Add other vegetables of your choice, such as chopped celery, leeks, carrots or parsnips.

KIDNEYS SAUTÉD WITH BACON

as a frypan

Sautéd kidneys should be cooked for only 5 minutes, no longer, otherwise they must be treated as Braised Kidneys (*pp. 124–5*).

2 lambs' kidneys per serving
1 dessertspoon oil, butter or
  margarine

1 or more rashers of bacon per
  serving
salt and pepper

1 Prepare kidneys as described in step 1, p. 124. After removing fat and core, snip the middle of the round side of each kidney to prevent curling.
2 Meanwhile, put fat into Cooker and turn heat to 300 (3).
3 Remove rinds from bacon and put rashers into Cooker.
4 Fry for 1 minute, then add kidneys and fry for $2\frac{1}{2}$ minutes only on each side, (*see above*). Sprinkle with salt and pepper and serve at once with the bacon.

Kidneys sautéd with tomatoes, mushrooms and bacon: The tomatoes may be skinned or not, as preferred. Cut in halves and sprinkle with salt, pepper and a few grains of sugar. Put into the Cooker with the bacon. Add washed, sliced mushrooms and push into one corner of the Cooker. Add the kidneys. Sprinkle mushrooms and kidneys with salt and pepper.

Kidney, sausage and tomato bake: Cook the sausages first (*see p. 121*), and when almost cooked add kidneys and tomatoes. See first variation.

Veal kidney sautéd with bacon: This comes in one mass, made up of many little segments. Slice through in $\frac{1}{2}$ in (1·25 cm) slices and fry as for lambs' kidneys.

Kidneys with scrambled egg: Prepare kidneys and mixture for scrambled egg (*p. 24*). Put 2 tablespoons butter or margarine into Cooker and turn heat to 300 (3). Fry kidneys first for $2\frac{1}{2}$ minutes on each side then push them to the far end of the Cooker. Now tilt the Cooker towards you and pour in the scrambled egg. Move about and cook until egg has almost set. Serve with the kidneys.

FIVE-MINUTE LIVER AND BACON

as a frypan

Liver, like kidneys, should be cooked either for a short flash-fry time, or slowly for a long time; see recipe on p. 130. It is usually sold ready skinned and sliced.

3 teaspoons margarine
2 or more rashers of bacon per serving
about 4–6 oz (125–175 g) liver per serving, skinned and cut
into ½ in (1·25 cm) slices
a little flour
salt and pepper
tomatoes (optional)

1 Put margarine into Cooker and turn heat to 300 (3).
2 Remove rinds from bacon and begin to fry.
3 Rinse and dry the liver and coat with flour.
4 Push bacon to one end of the Cooker, then raise heat to 340 (4). When light goes out, flash-fry the liver for no more than 2–2½ minutes on each side. Sprinkle with salt and pepper and serve with the bacon. Tomatoes, skinned and halved, may be cooked at the same time. Sprinkle with a little salt, pepper and sugar.

BRAINS, CRUMBED, WITH BACON

as a frypan

Brains are said to be the most easily digested and quickly assimilated of all foods. They are also delicious and make a tasty breakfast dish.

1 set of brains per serving
1 rounded tablespoon butter or
margarine
about 2 rashers of bacon per
serving

1 egg, beaten with 1 tablespoon
water and a little salt and
pepper
fine dry breadcrumbs or
wheatgerm

1 To prepare the brains, soak for 10 minutes in cold, salted water, then drain and boil gently in a little fresh water for 10 minutes. Drain and cool then cut into quarters or slices. All this could be done the night before.
2 Put half the butter or margarine into Cooker and turn to 300 (3). Remove rinds from bacon and begin to fry.
3 Dip brains first into egg then into breadcrumbs. Add the rest of the fat to the Cooker and push bacon to one end. Raise heat to 340 (4) and fry the brains until a golden brown. Serve with the bacon.

LIVER PÂTÉ

A basic recipe from which many delicious variations can take off. If the tin is lined with strips of streaky bacon, the pâté turns out attractively striped.

¼ lb (100 g) streaky bacon for pâté, extra rashers for lining the tin if liked

2 teaspoons butter or margarine

1 lb (½ kg) lambs', calves' or pigs' liver, sliced

1 medium-sized onion, peeled and quartered

1 crushed clove of garlic, or use garlic salt or powder (optional)

1 scant teaspoon thyme

1 egg, beaten

4 tablespoons cream or evaporated milk

salt and pepper

1 Remove rinds (if any) from bacon and cut into 2 in (5 cm) pieces. Fry in a saucepan with the butter or margarine for 2 minutes.

2 Cut liver into pieces and fry with the bacon, then add onion. Fry all together for about 4 minutes without burning. Remove from heat.

3 Use a 1 lb (½ kg) loaf tin, metal or freezer foil, or a deep 7 in (17·5 cm) round cake tin. It could be lined on the bottom and part way up the sides with streaky bacon (*see above*).

4 Put rack in Cooker and turn heat to 420 (6).

5 Mince or blend the liver, bacon and onion, adding garlic if liked. If mincing, add thyme, egg, cream and seasoning afterwards. If blending, put all these ingredients into the blender goblet together. Blend or mince finely.

6 Press mixture into tin and cover with a piece of foil. Place on rack and cover with Cooker lid. Close vent and reduce heat to 340 (4). Allow 1 hour. Turn out.

Chicken liver pâté: Use chicken livers.

Liver and sausage pâté: Add ½ lb (225 g) sausage meat.

Veal and ham pâté: Use half veal and half ham.

Pâté with brandy: Add 1 tablespoon brandy after mincing or blending.

PORTUGUESE LIVER CASSEROLE

The bacon, tomato and sage combine to give this recipe a special flavour and might tempt even those who think they don't like liver. If possible, use an enamel or other metal casserole. It will fry well and save time. For more servings, use a larger casserole or see cook-and-serve method below.

½–¾ lb (225–250 g) lambs' or pigs' liver

1 or 2 rashers of streaky bacon, rinds removed

1 onion and 1 carrot, peeled and chopped (or use frozen mixed vegetables)

½–1 clove of garlic, well crushed (optional)

1 level tablespoon packet soup-mix (tomato-flavour)

½ beef stock cube

¼ pint (150 ml) hot water

1 teaspoon sage

salt and pepper

1 Cut liver into ½ in (1·25 cm) slices if not already sliced.
2 Put casserole dish (*see above*) into cold Cooker and set at 420 (6).
3 Cut bacon into 2 in (5 cm) pieces and drop into dish. Fry for a few minutes, then add vegetables, and garlic if liked, and continue frying for 3 minutes. Put in liver and move about until seared.
4 Stir soup mix and crumbled beef cube into water, then stir into casserole. Add sage and season with a little salt and pepper.
5 When gravy begins to simmer, reduce heat to 300 (3). Cover with casserole lid, then with Cooker lid. Close vent. Cook gently for about 1 hour or until tender.

As a cook-and-serve dish for more servings: Increase the ingredients proportionately. Put bacon into Cooker and turn heat to 300 (3). Fry the bacon, then the vegetables, then add garlic and liver. Increase liquid to 1 pint (575 ml) and make sure that it is hot. Add stock cube, sage and seasoning. Lower heat to 220 (1). Cover with Cooker lid and close vent. Cook gently for about 1 hour, or until liver is very tender. Add more water if necessary. Lastly add the packet soup-mix and stir until gravy has thickened.

3

Puddings and Pies
Fruit Dishes

This is a chapter of delicious sweet-course dishes, some well known, others appearing for the first time.

Many have either a meringue or a type of 'marshmallow' topping and an electric mixer will greatly reduce the work involved in the beating of the mixtures. However, all except the 'honey marshmallow' topping can be beaten by hand (traditionalists prefer meringue made entirely by the hand method as an exceptionally light result is obtained).

Meringue: whisk the whites until they stand in soft peaks, then whisk in one tablespoon of sugar until the whites are stiff. Finally, lightly but thoroughly fold in the remaining sugar 2 level tablespoons at a time.

'Marshmallow': whisk the whites to a soft peak, then whisk in first a tablespoon of sugar until stiff, followed by half the remaining sugar. Finally, lightly but thoroughly fold in the rest of the sugar 2 level tablespoons at a time, sprinkling in the cornflour, vinegar and salt with the last of the sugar.

With both mixtures the gentle folding keeps the whites stiff so that the finished result is as light as possible.

APPLE RICE MARSHMALLOW

A 'marshmallow' topping uses less sugar than a meringue and sets in less time. This is a three-layered sweet. On the bottom, creamed rice; in the middle, sweetened cooked apple, lemon flavoured; and on top, the marshmallow, either pink or white (*see Note*).

1½ cups canned sweetened stewed apple with 3 tablespoons lemon juice and sugar to taste, or home-cooked, using 1 lb (½ kg) peeled sliced apples with 3 tablespoons lemon juice, 4–5 rounded tablespoons sugar and 2 tablespoons water

2 egg yolks
1 lb (450 g) can of creamed rice

'MARSHMALLOW'
2 egg whites
3 level tablespoons sugar
1 good teaspoon cornflour
2 teaspoons vinegar
¼ level teaspoon salt

1 Prepare the apple with lemon juice, sugar, and water if home-cooked.
2 Use a heatproof dish, about 2½–3 in (7 cm) deep.
3 Beat yolks into the rice and tip into dish. Place on rack in Cooker and turn heat to 420 (6).
4 Cover rice with the apple.
5 Make marshmallow. Beat egg whites, sugar, cornflour, vinegar and salt with electric mixer until mixture stands stiffly in peaks. If you have no mixer, see p. 131.
6 Pile the marshmallow on top of the apple. Cover with Cooker lid and open vent. Cook for 35 minutes or until marshmallow is firm but still soft.

Note: For a pale pink marshmallow, add a few drops of cochineal to the marshmallow mixture before beating. The colour becomes paler as the mixture is beaten so add more cochineal for a more pronounced pink colour. It would make a pretty dessert for a children's party.

Peach or apricot rice marshmallow with liqueur: Replace the apple with canned peaches or apricots, drained and sliced. If using peaches sprinkle 2 tablespoons lemon juice, 1 tablespoon castor sugar and 1 tablespoon peach brandy over the fruit. If using apricots omit lemon juice and use 1 tablespoon apricot brandy. Cover with the rice then with the marshmallow.

APPLE CHARLOTTE

The old-fashioned recipe as recorded by Mrs Beeton was made in a pie dish lined with butter-soaked slices of bread, but today the fashion favours breadcrumbs instead. Here the more modern version is followed by the old-fashioned one.

2 tablespoons butter or margarine	*1 lb (½ kg) cooking apples*
4 oz (100 g), or 2 cups, fresh breadcrumbs (wholemeal for the health-conscious)	*4 oz (100 g) brown sugar*
	2 tablespoons lemon juice
	6 tablespoons water

1. Melt butter or margarine and stir in breadcrumbs, coating well.
2. Put a pie dish or other heatproof dish into cold Cooker and set heat at 420 (6).
3. Peel and slice the apples finely.
4. Put one-third of the buttered breadcrumbs into a dish and cover with half the apples. Sprinkle with half the sugar.
5. Cover with another third of the breadcrumbs then the rest of the apples and sugar. Spoon over the lemon juice and the water.
6. Top with the rest of the breadcrumbs. Cover with Cooker lid and close vent. Allow about 45 minutes, or until apples are mushy and top is slightly browned.

Old-fashioned version: Follow the above recipe, but instead of the breadcrumbs line the pie dish on the bottom and sides with slices of bread brushed generously with melted butter or margarine. Fill with the apples, sugar, lemon juice and water, then cover completely with more bread slices, overlapping. When cooked it is usually turned out on to a flat serving dish.

Blackberry or raspberry and apple Charlotte: Use half blackberries or raspberries and half apples or any combination. Omit lemon juice.

Tomato and apple Charlotte: Use 3 skinned sliced tomatoes with 12 oz (350 g) apples. Reduce water to 3 tablespoons. Include lemon juice.

APPLE PIE, DEEP-DISH

The pie will finish attractively if the pastry is first brushed over with
evaporated milk. The rest of the can may be used instead of cream
or to make yoghurt (*see p. 20*).

½ lb (*225 g*) *short pastry* (p. 193)   4 *tablespoons sugar for cooking*
1 lb (*½ kg*) *either cooking or eating*   *apples, 3 for eating apples*
    apples, peeled and sliced   4 *cloves*
                                           6 *tablespoons water*

1 Use a deep 7–8 in (18 cm) round pie dish, or a 9 in (22·5 cm)
   oval one.
2 Roll out pastry.
3 Put rack in Cooker and heat to 420 (6) with vent closed.
4 Put pie funnel or egg cup into pie dish and add sliced apples,
   sugar, cloves and liquid.
5 Wet edge of dish and put a 1 in (2·5 cm) strip of pastry around.
   Wet that, then cover dish with the rest of the pastry. Neaten edge
   and decorate. Make two slits to allow steam to escape and brush
   with evaporated milk (*see above*).
6 Place on rack, cover with Cooker lid and open vent. Leave heat
   at 420 (6) and allow 45–50 minutes. Try not to peep before
   40 minutes.

Note: The juice may be slightly thickened by the addition of 1 good
teaspoon small sago (not tapioca).

Orange apple pie, deep-dish: Replace 3 tablespoons of the water
with orange juice.

Marmalade apple pie, deep-dish: Replace 2 tablespoons of the
water with 3 tablespoons marmalade, and add 1 level teaspoon
ground cinnamon.

BAKED APPLES

As a rule baked apples need expensive oven heat but in the Cooker only an economical amount is required. The syrup must be simmered very gently. The sago thickening provides 'body' to the syrup and will dissolve completely.

1 pint (575 ml) water
2 tablespoons golden syrup
3 tablespoons lemon juice
1 tablespoon brown sugar

1 level dessertspoon small sago
  (not tapioca)
4 large apples, eating or cooking
Filling (see below)
a little butter

1 Pour water into Cooker. Add syrup, lemon juice, sugar and sago. Do not heat yet.
2 Core apples but do not make a hole right through: leave about ¼ in (0·5 cm) base to support the filling.
3 Make the filling, see below.
4 Set Cooker at 220 (1).
5 With a sharp knife cut a line round the circumference of each apple, through the skin only. This prevents the apples bursting.
6 Fill cored-out hollows with your chosen filling and top each apple with about ½ teaspoon butter. Place apples in the syrup.
7 Cover with Cooker lid and close vent. Allow 12–15 minutes. Baste twice. Reduce heat if boiling too quickly.

FILLINGS

Dried fruit: Use 2 oz (50 g) raisins, sultanas or a mixture of dried fruits. A little cinnamon or other spice could be added. After filling hollows add ½ teaspoon brown sugar as well as the topping of butter.

Fruit and nuts: Add 1 oz (25 g) chopped walnuts to the dried fruit mixture above.

Dates and lemon juice: Chop 2 oz (50 g) stoned dates and heat in a small saucepan with 2 tablespoons lemon juice. When just boiling remove from heat and add 1 teaspoon sugar. Beat until mushy.

APPLE CRUMBLE OR CRISP

Many generations of men and boys have 'asked for more' when apple crumble comes on as 'afters' and no doubt many generations in the future will do the same. The crisp crumbly topping is a rival to the pastry of apple pie and many declare it the winner. A few variations follow.

1 lb (½ kg) cooking apples, peeled and finely sliced
2 tablespoons lemon juice
4 level tablespoons sugar
2 tablespoons water

TOPPING
3 heaped tablespoons flour
¼ teaspoon salt
2 oz (50 g) butter or margarine
2 level tablespoons light soft brown sugar
1 rounded teaspoon cinnamon

1 Put rack in Cooker and heat to 420 (6).
2 Use a heatproof pie dish or soufflé dish, about 6½ in (16·25 cm) across. Put in the apples and add lemon juice and sugar. Put on rack in Cooker while crumble is being made.
3 Put flour and salt into a bowl and rub in the butter until mixture is crumbly (or use a mixer). Add sugar and cinnamon.
4 Spread this mixture on top of the apples. Cover with Cooker lid and open vent.
5 Allow 10 minutes at 420 (6) then reduce heat to 380 (5). Cook for another 25 minutes or until top is crisp.

Gooseberry crumble: Top and tail about 1 lb (½ kg) ripe gooseberries. Put into dish with 2 tablespoons water and 6 level tablespoons sugar. Proceed then with the recipe.

Crumble with muesli: Instead of the topping given in the main recipe, use 4 heaped tablespoons muesli. (See recipe for Homemade Muesli on p. 19.) A little more brown sugar could be added.

Pastry-mix crumble: This saves the bother of mixing in the fat. To 3 heaped tablespoons of short-pastry mix add 2 level tablespoons light soft brown sugar.

APPLE SPONGE

A popular family pudding. A sponge mixture is poured on to hot stewed apple and baked until light and golden.

1–1½ lb (½–¾ kg) apples, stewed with sugar and lemon juice, or canned apple sauce

SPONGE
1 egg
4 oz (100 g) sugar
4 oz (100 g) self-raising flour
¼ teaspoon salt
1 oz (25 g) butter or margarine
1 tablespoon golden syrup
2 tablespoons water

1 Use a 6–6½ in (16 cm) heatproof dish about 2½–3 in (7 cm) deep. Tip the hot apple into dish.

2 Put rack in Cooker and heat to 420 (6). Place dish on rack to keep apple hot.

3 Make sponge. Beat together the egg and sugar. Sieve the dry ingredients. Melt together the butter or margarine, golden syrup and water.

4 Add this alternately with the dry ingredients to the beaten egg and sugar. Stir well but do not beat. Pour this mixture over the hot apple.

5 Cover with Cooker lid and open vent. Cook at 420 (6) for 1 hour.

Note: To reheat remainder of pudding next day (if it has not already been demolished), put it on the rack in the Cooker, turn to 420 (6) and cover with Cooker lid. Allow about 10–15 minutes. The sponge will again be light and moist.

Plum sponge: At step 1, cook 1 lb (450 g) plums with 4–6 oz (100–175 g) sugar and 6 tablespoons water. One good teaspoon of small sago (not tapioca) will thicken the syrup slightly.

Gooseberry sponge: At step 1 cook 1 lb (450 g) topped and tailed ripe gooseberries with 4 tablespoons water and 6 oz (175 g) sugar. One teaspoon small sago (not tapioca) will thicken the syrup slightly.

CRISP APPLE DUMPLINGS

In the days when stomachs could take heavier food than today, the apples were wrapped in a suet crust and cooked in cloths in boiling water. In the recipe below, the pastry is short and thin and the dumplings baked until crisp.

¾ lb (350 g) short pastry, bought or homemade (p. 193)

4 or 5 medium-sized eating apples, about 4 oz (100 g) each

filling of sultanas, raisins or mixed dried fruits

sugar

1 Have either a double thickness of foil or a shallow tray or tin on which to cook the dumplings. Grease well. Place on floor of Cooker.

2 Roll out the pastry very thinly.

3 First core then peel the apples. If they are large cut in halves crosswise.

4 Fill hollows with sultanas or other dried fruits. Top with a little sugar.

5 Turn heat to 420 (6). Cut 6 in (15 cm) rounds of pastry with a saucer or lid and wrap one around each apple, or half apple. Seal well.

6 Place on foil or tin with the pastry join downwards. Cover with Cooker lid and open vent. Allow 45 minutes. Try not to look before 40 minutes are up.

Note: While the dumplings are cooking, syrup could be made by boiling together 2 level tablespoons golden syrup, the grated rind and juice of 1 lemon (or use commercial lemon juice and no rind), and 2 level teaspoons sago. Boil gently until sago has dissolved completely. Don't use seed tapioca—it doesn't dissolve as readily.

FRIED APPLE DUSKY PUDDING

The idea for this pudding first came to me while I was frying apple rings to serve with sausages (*p. 122*). Possibilities emerged and the ingredients suggested themselves. The result is the recipe below.

1 lb (½ kg) eating apples,
*   preferably red*
1 rounded tablespoon butter or
*   margarine*
¼ pint (150 ml) milk
2 level tablespoons golden syrup

1 rounded teaspoon cornflour
¼ teaspoon cinnamon
2 standard eggs
sprinkling of coconut (optional)
*   (see Note)*

1 Wash apples, then core, but do not peel. Put into cold water to prevent discolouring.
2 Put fat into Cooker and set heat at 340 (4).
3 Cut apples into ½ in (1·25 cm) rings. When light goes out fry until browned on both sides, about 5–6 minutes altogether.
4 Arrange apple rings in a deep 6–6½ in (16 cm) dish.
5 Heat the milk with the golden syrup. Mix the cornflour and cinnamon with 1 tablespoon water and stir in. Cook and stir until smooth. Remove from heat.
6 Wash Cooker with soapy water, then pour in 1½ pints (850 ml) fresh water. Heat to 220 (1) or gently boiling.
7 Beat the eggs and stir into sauce. Pour over the apples. Put dish into water and place a piece of foil on top. Cover with lid and close vent. Allow 30 minutes. When cooked, the top may be sprinkled with coconut, plain or toasted (*see Note*).

Note: Coconut, when toasted, takes on a more attractive appearance and better flavour. It may be toasted in bulk in advance and kept in a jar. Put about 4 oz (100 g) into the Cooker and turn to 340 (4) or a little higher. Cook until lightly browned. Stir continuously as it burns easily. For toasting on top of the pudding, put under a hot grill until golden.

ALMOND STUFFED PEACHES

as a poacher

serves 4

These may be served as a sweet or arranged around baked ham as an elegant garnish. For the sweet, the peaches are cooked in a silky sauce. See Note for stuffed peaches used as ham garnish.

4 large peaches
1 pint (575 ml) water
2 rounded teaspoons small sago
  (not tapioca)
3 level tablespoons light brown
  sugar
2 tablespoons lemon juice
1 tablespoon golden syrup
1 teaspoon vanilla flavouring
a few glacé cherries

FILLING
4 level tablespoons ground
  almonds
1 level tablespoon castor sugar
¼ teaspoon almond essence
a little sherry to form a paste

1 Rub the peaches with a scotch pad or other abrasive to take off the bloom. Halve and stone.
2 Pour water into Cooker and set at 220 (1). Add sago, sugar, lemon juice, golden syrup and vanilla flavouring.
3 Put in the peach halves and spoon over the sauce to baste.
4 Cover with Cooker lid and close vent. Turn heat down to Simmer and cook gently for 5–10 minutes or until peaches have softened.
5 Mix together the ingredients for the filling.
6 Lift out peaches and fill hollows. Top each with a glacé cherry. Place on a serving dish and pour the syrup around.

Note: If using the filled peaches to garnish ham, choose canned halves. Drain from the syrup in the can, fill hollows and heat through. If cooking the ham in the Cooker, remove and keep hot, then put the peaches on the rack. Cover with lid and heat with Cooker set at 340 (4).

PEARS AND PRUNES

The prunes may be served with the pears, or used decoratively in the pear hollows as either a dessert or an accompaniment to pork or veal.

¼ lb (225 g), or more, uncooked prunes (see Note)
1 pint (575 ml) water
1 lb (½ kg) pears, peeled, halved and cored
2 tablespoons golden syrup

about 1 tablespoon brown sugar, according to taste
2 tablespoons lemon juice
1 rounded teaspoon small sago (not tapioca)
¼ teaspoon salt

1 Put prunes and cold water into Cooker and turn to 220 (1). Leave the prunes to soak while the pears are being prepared.
2 Put in the pears and add the golden syrup, sugar, lemon juice, sago and salt.
3 Cover with Cooker lid and close vent.
4 Turn heat down to a simmering point that will allow only gentle cooking. Cooking time will depend on the hardness of the pears. Reduce syrup to about ½ pint (275 ml).

Note: If prunes are to be used to fill the pear hollows only, use 1 prune for each pear half. Remove stones.

Pears Creole with prunes: Add 1 teaspoon ground ginger, ½ teaspoon ground nutmeg and ½ teaspoon cinnamon to the syrup at step 2.

Pears and prunes with port wine: Substitute white sugar for brown and 10 minutes before cooking time is up add 4–6 tablespoons port wine. This will deepen the colour of the pears.

APRICOT AND PRUNE UPSIDE-DOWN PUDDING

When the pudding has been cooked and the time comes for turning it out, you will have the pleasure of seeing the pattern you had arranged on the bottom decorating the top, enhanced by the sheen of the syrup and butter you had first poured into the dish.

1 rounded tablespoon butter or margarine
1 tablespoon golden syrup
about 8 each of apricots and prunes, dried (soaked and cooked) or canned and stoned (proportions of these fruits can vary)
glacé cherries

SPONGE
1 large egg
5 oz (150 g) sugar
2 oz (50 g) butter or margarine
4 tablespoons water
5 oz (150 g) self-raising flour
¼ teaspoon salt

1 In a small saucepan melt together the butter or margarine and the golden syrup. Pour this into a 7½–8 in (19 cm) cake tin about 1½–2 in (4–5 cm) deep.
2 Arrange the apricots (hollow side down) and prunes in a pattern on the bottom.
3 Put rack in Cooker and heat to 420 (6).
4 For the sponge, begin by beating together the egg and sugar until light.
5 Melt the butter or margarine with the water in the same small saucepan.
6 Sieve the flour and salt and add to egg mixture, stir in the melted butter. Stir everything together but do not beat.
7 Pour this mixture on to the prune and apricot pattern and spread evenly. Place on rack and cover with Cooker lid. Open vent. Reduce heat to 380 (5) and allow 1 hour 10 minutes. Have a look after 1 hour.
8 Turn out on to a flat dish, then put a glacé cherry into the hollow of each apricot.

Pineapple and cherry upside-down pudding: Use pineapple and canned or fresh pitted cherries. Pineapple slices may be arranged in halves around a complete ring. Put cherries into centres in any pattern you wish.

PANCAKES

Pancakes are eaten on all sorts of occasions all the year round, but they have a special part to play on one day of the year: Shrove Tuesday, the day before Ash Wednesday and the Lenten fast.

5 oz (150 g) plain flour
1 oz (25 g) cornflour
1 level teaspoon salt
2 rounded teaspoons sugar
1 egg

½ pint (275 ml) milk
¼ pint (150 ml) water
1 tablespoon vegetable or corn oil
butter or margarine

1 Sieve flour, cornflour and salt into a mixing bowl. Add sugar.
2 Beat egg in a small bowl and add milk and water. Stir this into the flour, then add oil and beat until smooth. The mixture should be as thin as single cream, so add a little more water if necessary. The pancakes are improved if the mixture is left to stand for half an hour or longer before cooking, but this is not essential. Pour into a jug.
3 Drop 1 good teaspoon butter or margarine into Cooker and heat to 340 (4). When butter has melted, brush the base of the Cooker with it.
4 When light has gone out, begin to cook the pancakes. Pour from a height of about 8 in (20 cm) into the centre of the Cooker until a 6 or 7 in (16 cm) thin pancake is formed. Cook on one side until bubbles appear then flip over and cook on the other side until lightly browned.
5 The pancakes may be rolled at once and kept warm, then unrolled to be either served with lemon and sugar, or filled with a sweet or savoury mixture. Alternatively, they may be left flat and piled on top of each other with greaseproof paper or thin foil in between.

Apple and lemon juice pancakes: Grate 3 large sweet apples and add 4 level tablespoons castor sugar and 3 tablespoons lemon juice (if fresh lemon is used, add zest also). Spread a little on each pancake and roll up.

Pineapple and cream cheese pancakes: Follow method above, using 2 cups finely chopped pineapple mixed with 4 oz (100 g) cream cheese.

CRÊPES SUZETTES

If you have had Crêpes Suzettes at a restaurant, you will have
noticed that the chef cooks the sauce and flames the liqueur or
brandy on a chafing dish heated from underneath. The Multi Cooker
also has heat underneath which can be easily regulated. So if you
have a point near your dining-table or an extension flex, you could
do the same.

12 very thin 6 in (15 cm)
  Pancakes (p. 143)
1 large orange
2 tablespoons butter

3 level tablespoons light soft
  brown sugar
4 tablespoons curaçao or
  cointreau

1 Make the pancakes.
2 Put them into two stacks of six each, with greaseproof paper or
   thin wrapping foil between each. Keep warm. If they have been
   made the day before, they could be warmed on the rack in the
   Cooker.
3 Grate the orange rind, using just the outer, yellow skin. Squeeze
   out the juice.
4 Put butter in Cooker and heat to 300 (3). When butter begins to
   melt add the sugar. Cook together for 2 minutes. Add orange
   juice and rind. Lower heat so that the juice is simmering very
   gently. The mixture should not boil.
5 Lay a pancake in the mixture, then straight away fold it in four
   and put to the end of the pan. Repeat with the rest of the pancakes
   then move them into the middle of the Cooker and pour in the
   liqueur. Wait half a minute to make sure it is hot, then set it
   alight. Serve pancakes with sauce poured over.

FRITTERS, SWEET

as a frypan

Fat: See p. 50.

Fritter batter: See recipe on p. 50, but add 1 rounded dessertspoon sugar.

Apple fritters: Core sweet eating apples and peel, if preferred. Cut into $\frac{1}{2}$ in (1·25 cm) slices. Heat fat. Dip slices in batter and fry until a golden brown on both sides, about 4–5 minutes altogether. Drain on kitchen paper and dust with castor sugar.

Pineapple fritters: Use either canned pineapple rings or slices of fresh pineapple with hard centres removed. Proceed then as for apple fritters.

Pear fritters: Peel, quarter and remove cores. Brush with a little lemon juice to add flavour. Proceed then as for apple fritters.

Banana fritters: Peel bananas and if large cut in halves crosswise. Brush with lemon juice. Proceed then as for apple fritters. Delicious served with Caramel Rum Sauce (*p. 192*).

Prune and walnut fritters: Remove stones from cooked prunes and push half a walnut into each. Press closed. They may then be soaked for a few hours in lemon juice, wine (preferably port) or sherry before frying. Proceed then as for apple fritters.

BAKED CUSTARD

as a bain-marie *serves 3–4*

The boiling temperature of water is perfect for 'baked' custards. In the days of large kitchens when the bain-marie was part of the usual equipment, it was simple to cook custards in this 'bath'. Today, the same may be done in a Multi Cooker.

¾ *pint (425 ml) warm milk*
2 *level tablespoons sugar*
  or 1 tablespoon golden syrup

½ *teaspoon vanilla flavouring or*
  1 vanilla pod
2 *large eggs*
nutmeg

1 Use a soufflé or pie dish about 5–5½ in (13 cm) across and 3 in (7·5 cm) deep.
2 Put milk, sugar or golden syrup, and vanilla flavouring or pod into a small saucepan and heat. Do not let it get near boiling point.
3 Pour 1½ pints (¾ litre) water into Cooker and put in rack. Turn to 220 (1).
4 Remove milk from heat and take out pod if used. Beat the eggs very well and stir into milk.
5 Pour into dish, dust with nutmeg and stand on rack. Cover loosely with a piece of foil, then with Cooker lid. Close vent. Cook for 20 minutes. Reduce heat a little if water is boiling too fiercely, but don't let it go off the boil for long.

Caramel custard: To save time making the caramel (by boiling 3 rounded tablespoons sugar with 2 tablespoons water until light brown), see p. 192 to caramelize condensed milk. Put 2 tablespoons of caramel on the bottom of the dish, after greasing it, then continue with the above recipe.

Caramel custards, small: See Caramel Custard above. Use small ramekins, which are usually ¼ pint (150 ml) size. Put about 1 dessertspoon caramel sauce in each dish after greasing. Make custard as in main recipe and divide mixture between the ramekins. Allow 10 minutes' cooking time.

Caramel flavoured custard: Follow main recipe and instead of sugar or golden syrup, sweeten with caramel sauce. One tablespoon rum could be added.

BREAD AND BUTTER PUDDING

In the last century many households often had a surfeit of bread and this prompted the creation of many recipes to use up the left-overs. The quality of the bread and butter pudding depended on the skill of the cook. Too much bread and too little milk and eggs would have produced something that was more like a poultice than a pudding; but when the proportions were right the result was loved.

about 3½ oz (88 g) bread slices
  about ¼ in (0·5 cm) thick,
  buttered
2–3 oz (50–75 g) raisins or
  sultanas

½ pint (275 ml) milk
½ teaspoon vanilla flavouring or a
  vanilla pod
2 eggs
3 level tablespoons sugar

1 Cut bread into triangles and layer in a heatproof pie dish or soufflé dish about 6–6½ in (16 cm) across.
2 Scatter the fruit over the top.
3 Put rack in Cooker and heat to 420 (6).
4 Gently warm the milk in a small saucepan with the vanilla.
5 Beat the eggs with the sugar. Stir in the milk, removing vanilla pod if used. Pour over the bread and fruit.
6 Put dish on rack. Cover with Cooker lid and open vent. Cook for 10 minutes at 420 (6), then turn down to 340 (4) and cook for another 15 minutes, or until set.

Bread and butter pudding with sherry: At step 1 pour 2–4 tablespoons sherry over the bread.

Bread, butter and jam pudding: Spread bread with jam as well as butter. Sherry may also be added.

CARAMEL RUM MARSHMALLOW PIE
WITH WALNUTS

as an oven   *makes an 8 in (20 cm) pie*

Pure indulgence. A pie full of calories that weight-watchers will
have to avoid, though many will be tempted to have a *little*, just *once*!

Crumb Crust (made using 1 egg
  yolk) (p. 193)
½ pint (275 ml) milk, cream or
  evaporated milk
1 good tablespoon caramel
  (see Note)
2 rounded tablespoons brown
  sugar
2 level tablespoons cornflour
2 tablespoons rum
1 egg yolk

2 tablespoons coarsely chopped
  walnuts, or more if you wish
1 teaspoon vanilla flavouring

'MARSHMALLOW'
3 level tablespoons sugar
2 egg whites
1 rounded teaspoon cornflour
2 teaspoons vinegar
¼ level teaspoon salt

1 Make crumb crust and press into an 8 in (20 cm) dish, about
  1½ in (3·75 cm) deep. Put into refrigerator and when firm neaten
  edge.
2 Meanwhile, make filling. Heat milk with caramel and sugar in
  a saucepan. Mix cornflour with 2 tablespoons cold water until
  smooth and stir in. Cook and stir until thick. Remove from heat
  and add rum.
3 Beat in the egg yolk. Add walnuts and vanilla.
4 Put rack in Cooker and heat to 420 (6).
5 Remove crust from refrigerator and pour in the filling.
6 Make the marshmallow. With an electric mixer, beat the sugar,
  egg whites, cornflour, vinegar and salt. If you have no mixer,
  see p. 131. Beat until the mixture is stiff enough to stand in peaks,
  then pile on top of the filling.
7 Place dish on rack, cover with lid and open vent. Allow about 30
  minutes. The topping will be a soft marshmallow. Delicious
  served with whipped cream laced with 1 tablespoon rum or brandy
  and 1 teaspoon sugar.

Note: Either make your own caramel with sugar and water (*see
Caramel Custard p. 146*) or see p. 192 to caramelize condensed milk.

LEMON MERINGUE PIE

In the early editions of Mrs Beeton's cookery book, there's a recipe (or receipt) called Baked Lemon Pudding which could be the forerunner of our present-day lemon meringue pie. In even earlier times, it was called a lemon pudding-pie or pudden-pie and the whites of the eggs would have been discarded, using only the yolks. By 1912 a completely revised edition of the cookery book was published and here the whites were used to make a meringue topping. Below we given an even newer version, with a very lazy filling.

8 oz (225 g) bought or homemade
*　short pastry (p. 193)*

FILLING
a ¼ pint (150 ml) can of
*　sweetened condensed milk*
grated rind and juice of 2 lemons
2 egg yolks (standard)

MERINGUE
2 egg whites (standard)
4 rounded tablespoons sugar
¼ teaspoon salt

1 Make filling first. Combine condensed milk with the grated rind and juice of the lemons. Beat in the egg yolks. Leave to stand and thicken while the crust is being made.

2 Put rack in Cooker and heat to 420 (6).

3 Roll out pastry thinly. Wet edge of dish and put a 1 in (2·5 cm) strip around. Wet that, then line the dish. Neaten edge and decorate.

4 Stand on rack, cover with Cooker lid and open vent. Allow 20 minutes, until partly cooked.

5 Meanwhile, make meringue with electric mixer (contrary to the rules, I have found meringue can be made with the mixer by putting all the ingredients in together from the beginning, but you may prefer to begin with whites only until a soft peak is formed, then adding sugar and salt and beating to a stiff peak). If you have no mixer, see p. 131.

6 Pour filling into pie shell and top with the meringue. Spread or swirl evenly. Cover with Cooker lid and open vent. Reduce heat to 380 (5) and allow about 35–40 minutes, or until meringue is just crisp on top.

GINGER-CRUNCH MERINGUE PIE

This is a fruit-custard pie with a crust of crushed ginger biscuits.
They are also known as Black-bottom Pies.

Black-bottom Crumb Crust,
using ginger biscuits (p. 193)
a 1 lb (450 g) can of fruit, such as
pineapple, peaches, apricots
½ pint (275 ml) thick custard
either canned or made with
custard powder (see Note)
2 oz (50 g) chopped crystallized
ginger

2 tablespoons lemon juice and the
grated rind if fresh lemon is
used

MERINGUE
2 egg whites
4 rounded tablespoons sugar
¼ teaspoon salt

1 Line an 8 in (20 cm) dish about 1½ in (3·75 cm) deep with the
crumb crust mixture. Press in firmly, but neaten the edge after it
has hardened—it is more easily done then. Put into refrigerator.
2 Strain syrup from fruit. Chop and stir into custard. Add ginger
and lemon.
3 Put rack in Cooker and turn heat to 420 (6).
4 When separating the eggs to obtain the whites for the meringue,
drop the whites into a mixing bowl and the yolks into a cup or
small bowl. Cover yolks with cold water and put away in refrigerator to be used in another dish (the water prevents a skin forming
on the yolks).
5 See step 5 on p. 149 for how to make the meringue. If you have
no mixer, see p. 131.
6 Remove dish from refrigerator and tip in custard mixture. Pile
meringue on top. Place dish on rack and cover with lid. Open
vent. Allow about 35–40 minutes or until meringue is crisp on top.

Note: To make homemade custard—heat ½ pint (275 ml) milk in a
saucepan with 2 level tablespoons sugar and ¼ teaspoon salt. Mix 2
level tablespoons custard powder with 4 tablespoons cold water
until smooth. Remove milk from heat and stir in the custard powder.
Return to heat and cook and stir until smooth and thick. Add ½
teaspoon vanilla flavouring.

FARMHOUSE SWEET CHEESE PIE

Although this is often served in restaurants and sold in delicatessens as cheesecake, it originated centuries ago in the farmhouses of rural England. They already had the curd cheese, the eggs and the cream, and they mainly flavoured them with ground almonds or currants. Here we use lemon juice with almond and vanilla flavourings. The traditional ground almonds and currants could be added, or pineapple or other fruit.

Crumb Crust (p. 193)
2 eggs
2 rounded tablespoons sugar
¼ lb (225 g) curd or cream cheese, not cottage cheese
2 tablespoons lemon juice and the grated rind if fresh lemon is used

4 tablespoons single cream or top of the milk
¼ teaspoon salt
¼ teaspoon each of vanilla and almond flavouring

1 Use an 8 in (20 cm) pie dish about 1½ in (3·75 cm) deep.
2 Make crumb crust, first dropping the white of one of the eggs into a mixing bowl. Use the yolk in the crumb mixture. Press mixture into the dish to line, then put into refrigerator to harden for about 20 minutes.
3 Put rack in Cooker and heat to 420 (6).
4 To the egg white add the whole egg, sugar, cheese, lemon, cream or top of the milk, salt and flavourings. Beat well. Add any one of the additional ingredients if liked (*see below*).
5 Remove pie dish from refrigerator, neaten edge and pour in the creamy mixture.
6 Place on rack. Cover with lid and open vent. Reduce heat to 380 (5) and cook for about 30 minutes. Serve cold. The pie may be covered with whipped cream and decorated with almonds or fruit. A little brandy with 1 teaspoon sugar gives the whipped cream a delicious flavour.

Additions: 2 level tablespoons ground almonds; 2 tablespoons currants; or fruit, such as chopped pineapple or cherries.

FRUIT SPONGE WITH HONEY MARSHMALLOW

as an oven   *serves 4*

The base is made with left-over sponge cake soaked in fruit syrup and if you wish a few tablespoons of port wine or sherry. The topping is light and velvety.

about 6–8 oz (175–200 g) sponge
  cake
a 1 lb (½ kg) can of fruit, such as
  apricots, peaches, pears, or use
  stewed apple

4 tablespoons port wine or sherry
  (optional)
2 egg whites (see Note below)
2 rounded tablespoons sugar
1 tablespoon honey

1 Put the sponge cake into a heatproof dish, about 3 in (7·5 cm) deep.
2 Open can of fruit and pour syrup over cake. If wine or sherry is to be used, pour that over first and add the amount of syrup the cake will take.
3 Arrange the fruit on top. For mild-flavoured fruit, such as pears or peaches, add something sharp such as orange or mandarin segments, passionfruit or pitted grapes.
4 Put rack in Cooker and heat to 380 (5).
5 With electric mixer beat first the egg whites and sugar until beginning to stiffen, then add the honey and continue beating until it will stand in peaks. Pile on top of the pudding and place on rack. Cover with Cooker lid and open vent. Allow 20–25 minutes, or until firm but not crisp.

Note: Because of the honey an electric mixer is essential for this topping.

STRAWBERRY MARSHMALLOW WITH PORT WINE

A party piece that may be prepared well in advance.

1 lb (½ kg) strawberries
2 level tablespoons sugar
2 tablespoons port wine
1 level teaspoon sago
whipped cream

'MARSHMALLOW'

2 egg whites
4 level tablespoons sugar
1 teaspoon cornflour
2 teaspoons lemon juice
pinch salt

1 Use a heatproof dish about 6 in (15 cm) across and about 2 in (5 cm) deep.

2 Put rack in Cooker and heat to 420 (6). Put dish on to rack.

3 Hull strawberries and place in dish. Add sugar, port and sago. Cover with Cooker lid and open vent. Allow to heat while the 'marshmallow' is being made.

4 For marshmallow, put egg whites, sugar, cornflour, lemon juice and salt into bowl of electric mixer. Beat at highest speed until meringue will stand stiffly in peaks. If you have no mixer, see p. 131.

5 The strawberries should be boiling or very hot by now. Pour the meringue on top. Reduce heat to 340 (4). Cover with Cooker lid and open vent. Allow 25 minutes.

6 Lift out and allow to cool. The marshmallow will sink a little, but will still be about 1¼–1½ in (3 cm) high.

7 Top with whipped cream or serve cream separately.

Apple and lemon marshmallow: Use 1 lb (500 g) peeled sliced apples, 2 tablespoons lemon juice (and grated rind if using fresh lemon), 3–4 level tablespoons sugar, and the sago. Omit port wine.

Strawberry and pineapple marshmallow. Use ½ lb (225 g) strawberries and 1 small can of pineapple, cut into pieces. Omit port wine and use instead 2 tablespoons pineapple syrup.

Apple and tomato marshmallow: An interesting and delicious combination of flavours. Use ¾ lb (350 g) peeled sliced apples instead of the strawberries, and add 2 large or 3 small tomatoes, peeled and sliced. Allow 3 level tablespoons sugar. Omit port wine; the tomatoes will provide the liquid.

PINEAPPLE CUSTARD MARSHMALLOW

An old-fashioned pudding revived and given a 'marshmallow' topping instead of a meringue one. See below for a novel variation.

1 lb (½ kg) can of pineapple
¼ pint (150 ml) milk
1½ tablespoons golden syrup
2 level tablespoons cornflour
¼ pint (150 ml) pineapple syrup
3 tablespoons lemon juice and grated rind if possible
2 egg yolks

'MARSHMALLOW'
2 egg whites
3 rounded tablespoons sugar
¼ teaspoon salt
2 teaspoons vinegar
1 teaspoon cornflour

1 Drain off the syrup from the can of pineapple. Chop pineapple if in rings.
2 In a small saucepan heat the milk with the golden syrup, but do not boil yet.
3 Mix cornflour with the pineapple syrup and stir into milk. Cook and stir until thick, then add lemon rind and juice.
4 Remove from heat and beat in the egg yolks. Add pineapple.
5 Put rack in Cooker and heat to 380 (5).
6 For the marshmallow beat together the egg whites, sugar, salt, vinegar and cornflour, using an electric mixer. Beat until peaks will stand stiffly and not flop over. If you have no mixer, see p. 131.
7 Use a 7 in (18 cm) deep pie dish or soufflé dish and pour the pineapple custard into it. Top with marshmallow. Place on rack and cover with Cooker lid. Open vent. Allow 20–25 minutes or until marshmallow has set.

Honey marshmallow: Instead of 3 tablespoons sugar, add 2 tablespoons of sugar plus 1 of firm honey. Add the salt and cornflour, but instead of the vinegar use ¼ teaspoon cream of tartar. Because of the honey an electric mixer is essential for this topping.

PAVLOVA

A real Pavlova is not a meringue shell, hollowed in the middle, but a thick cake which, when cooked, is crisp meringue on the outside and a soft marshmallow inside. An essential part of the cake is the whipped cream, which counteracts some of the sweetness. It originated in New Zealand, then became popular in Australia.

4 egg whites	*¼ teaspoon salt*
8 oz (225 g) white sugar	*whipped cream*
1 heaped teaspoon cornflour	*pineapple or other fruit*
2 teaspoons vinegar	*brandy or rum (optional)*

1 Use a 9 in (22·5 cm) flat baking tray or tin, or use 2 thicknesses of smooth foil. Grease well.
2 Put egg whites, sugar, cornflour, vinegar and salt into bowl of electric mixer (*see p. 149, step 5*, on making meringue with electric mixer: cornflour and vinegar are added with the sugar). Beat at highest speed until mixture will stand in stiff peaks and not fall over. If you have no mixer, see p. 131.
3 Put rack in Cooker and heat to 380 (5). Place tray or foil on rack.
4 Pile the meringue mixture on to the tray in a high round about 6 in (15 cm) across. It will spread to about 8 in (20 cm).
5 Cover with Cooker lid and open vent. Reduce heat to 340 (4). Allow about 1¼ hours. When cooked the outside should be crisp and it should move easily on the tray. Slip on to a serving dish and when cold cover thickly with whipped cream, to which brandy or rum may be added, and garnish with fruit.

Meringues: Use the same ingredients as in step 2 of Pavlova recipe above. This quantity will make 32 meringues. Put rack in Cooker and heat to 380 (5). Place on the rack a shallow tray or doubled piece of smooth foil, or use a 10 in (25 cm) foil baking dish. Grease all well. Put the meringue mixture on the greased surface— 1 dessertspoon of mixture for each meringue. Cover with Cooker lid and open vent. For meringues that are to be soft inside allow 25 minutes. For meringues that are to be crisp all through allow about 45 minutes. Scoop out some of the under part and sandwich two together with whipped cream.

HONEY AND ORANGE RAISIN TART

as an oven   *makes an 8 in (20 cm) tart*

Scientists have discovered that honey is so pure that germs cannot live in it.

grated rind and juice of 1 large
   orange (see Note)
2 tablespoons honey, preferably
   runny
¼ pint (150 ml) water
1 level tablespoon cornflour

¼ teaspoon salt
about 6 oz (175 g), or 1 cup,
   raisins
8 oz (225 g) short pastry, bought
   or homemade (p. 193)

1 Put orange rind and juice into a saucepan with the honey and water. Begin to heat.
2 Mix cornflour with 2 tablespoons water and add the salt. Mix smoothly then stir into orange mixture. Cook and stir until smooth. Remove from heat. Add raisins.
3 Roll out the pastry thinly. Wet the edge of an 8 in (20 cm) shallow pie plate or other suitable tart dish. A freezer foil container would do. Cut a 1 in (2·5 cm) strip of pastry and put around the edge. Wet that, then line the dish. Neaten edge and decorate.
4 Put rack in Cooker and heat to 420 (6).
5 Tip raisin mixture into tart. To make a lattice topping, cut strips of pastry ½ in (1·25 cm) wide, twist, then put criss-cross fashion on top of the filling.
6 When Cooker light goes out, put in the tart. Cover with Cooker lid and open vent. Allow 35 minutes. Try not to look before 30 minutes are up.

Note: If an orange is put into boiling water for a few minutes, then cooled under the cold tap, it will be easier to grate and juicier. When grating make sure you don't include the white pith.

FELIXSTOWE TART

In New Zealand this recipe is in the cookbooks as 'Felixtown Tart'. It proved a successful recipe in the Multi Cooker, but I felt that before giving it I ought to find out where Felixtown is. In all the world there did not seem to be a place called Felixtown. Then by a strange coincidence I saw the same recipe in an old handwritten receipt book belonging to my English grandmother—it was called 'Felixstowe Tart'. Evidently the title had been changed by a slip of pen or printer.

2 oz (50 g) butter or margarine	*2 oz (50 g) self-raising flour*
1 rounded tablespoon sugar	*¼ teaspoon salt*
1 teaspoon hot water	*1 rounded tablespoon castor sugar*
1 egg, separated	*about 4 tablespoons jam*
1 rounded tablespoon cornflour	

1 Cream the butter and sugar with the hot water.

2 Put rack in Cooker and heat to 420 (6). Use a shallow 7 in (17·5 cm) pie plate. A foil one would do.

3 Add egg yolk to creamed mixture and mix well, then stir in the cornflour, flour and salt. Mix to a dough and roll out. Place on the plate and neaten the edge. Mark with a fork all round to decorate.

4 Place on rack, cover with Cooker lid and open vent. Cook for 20–25 minutes.

5 Beat egg white until very stiff and fold in the castor sugar.

6 Remove tart and spread with jam, then cover with the meringue. Put back into Cooker, reduce heat to 380 (5) and cook for a further 15 minutes.

TREACLE TART

The traditional title 'Treacle Tart' has not yet given way to 'Golden Syrup Tart', though today the stronger flavoured treacle is seldom used for the filling. Plenty of breadcrumbs and a little lemon juice reduce the sweetness.

6 oz (175 g) short pastry, bought or homemade (p. 193)
3 good tablespoons golden syrup
3 heaped tablespoons fresh breadcrumbs

1 tablespoon lemon juice, with grated rind if using a fresh lemon

1 Put rack in Cooker and heat to 420 (6).
2 Roll out pastry thinly and line a 7 in (17·5 cm) shallow pie dish or plate or use a foil tart container.
3 Neaten edge and decorate with fingers and thumb, or in any way you choose.
4 Mix together the syrup, crumbs and lemon and spread into tart. (*See Note.*)
5 Stand on rack, cover with Cooker lid and open vent. Allow 35 minutes.

Note: To make a lattice of squares or diamonds, cut long ½ in (1·25 cm) wide strips of pastry, twist and place about 1 in (2·5 cm) apart on top of the filling, first across one way then at right angles the other way.

Jam tart: Use jam instead of syrup. Omit the breadcrumbs. Lemon could be included but is not usual.

4

Yeast Cooking
Baking Powder Loaves, Muffins, Doughnuts and Scones
Cakes
Tarts and Biscuits

With a Multi Cooker, all these recipes are available to you. The heat will not be as high as that in a conventional oven, so a little more time is needed for the cooking. Browning is usually no more than a pale gold on top, but this does not affect the taste or texture. If you wish to remedy this, cakes may be iced, and buns, loaves and rolls may be browned for a few minutes under a grill.

Notes on Yeast Cooking

In early times, before baking powder was 'invented', yeast was the rising agent for bread, cakes and some puddings made in the home. It is usual to see in our very old 'Books of Receipts' the instruction: 'Put on the hearth near a warm fire to rise.'

The living yeast: Yeast cooking is not difficult, but yeast is a living thing and, like the rest of us, needs to be *understood*. It will work away at a lump of dough, reproducing itself and at the same time puffing it up with air (or gas if you like). But it cannot make the process work without the right conditions.

No excesses please: The liquid used for mixing the yeast dough should be lukewarm or blood heat. Excessive heat kills yeast. During the first rising, the dough should double its bulk and the time taken for this will depend on two things: the amount of yeast used in the dough and the temperature of the air surrounding it. Excesses of either will cause the dough to rise too quickly, resulting in a coarse, poor-textured bread.

Amounts: 1 oz (25 g) caked yeast will leaven 3 lb (1½ kg) flour. ½ oz (13 g) dried yeast will leaven the same amount. See instructions on the packet. Less yeast may be used, but the dough will take longer to rise. It is unwise to go the other way and use too much yeast (*see previous paragraph*).

Temperatures: It is not necessary to worry about exact temperatures for rising. The dough will work at any temperature from 60° F (15° C) to 88° F (30° C). The lower the temperature, the longer the dough takes to rise. At 75–88° F (24–30° C) it will take about 2 hours. In a coolish kitchen (60° F, 15° C), the dough could be left to rise all night. If it is warmer, do not risk it. The yeast will work away to its limit, then collapse with exhaustion, never to rise again.

Using the Multi Cooker for rising: Put bowl with dough on rack and cover tightly with foil. Cover with lid and close vent. Turn the control slowly from the 'off' position and stop as soon as the light comes on. Leave it there. Allow 2 hours for the dough to double in bulk. Do not turn heat off. It will be needed for the second rising.

HOME-BAKED YEAST BREAD

If you have a Multi Cooker but no oven, you won't be denied the satisfaction of making your own bread. The whole process from rising to final baking may be done in the Cooker; see Notes on Yeast Cooking (*p. 160*).

½ oz (*13 g*) *caked yeast or 2 level teaspoons dried yeast*	*3 level teaspoons salt*
1 teaspoon sugar	*a little over ½ pint (275 ml) warm water, or half water and half milk*
4 tablespoons warm water	
1½ lb (675 g) strong bread flour	*1 tablespoon melted butter or margarine (optional)*

1 *Caked yeast:* put into a cup with the sugar and stir until it forms a liquid. Add the 4 tablespoons warm water (a little warmer than tepid). *Dried yeast:* put into a cup with the sugar and the 4 tablespoons warm water. Leave for about 10 minutes to work.

2 Sieve flour and salt into a large mixing bowl. Make a well in the centre and pour in the yeast. Mix in a little flour and leave for 10 minutes until it froths. This is called 'sponging' and gives the yeast a good start.

3 Now begin to mix into a dough, adding the warm liquid—a little more will almost certainly be needed. Add also butter or margarine if liked. Mix well and leave the dough in the bowl.

4 Put rack into Cooker and place bowl on it. Cover it tightly with foil. See p. 160: 'Using the Multi Cooker for rising'.

5 Meanwhile, grease well either one 2 lb (1 kg) or two 1 lb (½ kg) loaf tins. Both sizes are available in foil containers.

6 In about 2 hours, the dough will have doubled in bulk and be ready for kneading. Tip dough out on to a floury surface and knead for 8 or more minutes (the longer the better). Put into tin or tins and place on rack in Cooker. Cover with lid and open vent. Allow dough to rise until it comes to the top of the loaf tin, about 40 minutes. Turn heat up to 300 (3) for 15 minutes, then to 420 (6) until cooked. A large loaf will need about 45–50 minutes and the small ones about 35–40 minutes. When cooked they will sound hollow if tapped.

Wholemeal bread: Use half white and half wholemeal flour, or any proportion you wish.

FROZEN BREAD DOUGH

The loaves are usually sold in pairs. Grease two 1 lb ($\frac{1}{2}$ kg) loaf tins (foil tins are available in 1 and 2 lb ($\frac{1}{2}$ and 1 kg) sizes), and put in frozen dough. Leave at room temperature for about an hour to partially thaw. Put rack in Cooker and turn control slowly from the 'off' position until the light comes on. Leave it there. Put tins on rack and cover with Cooker lid. Close vent. Let the dough rise to the top of the tins, then turn heat to 420 (6) and open vent. Cook for about 35–40 minutes or until loaves sound hollow when tapped. The top will not be as brown as oven-baked bread, but it will taste just as good.

FROZEN BREAD ROLLS

Again only one rising is necessary before cooking. Have a shallow, rectangular, square or round cake tin, or use foil baking tins. Grease well. The rolls should be placed about $\frac{3}{4}$ in (2 cm) apart so that they will touch each other when they rise, and cook together. If you use a round tin, place one roll in the centre and arrange the others around. They can then be broken apart after cooking. Put rack in Cooker and place rolls on it. Turn control slowly from the 'off' position until the light comes on. Leave it there. Allow rolls to rise to almost double their size. Open vent and turn to 420 (6). Allow 25–30 minutes. While hot, brush with butter or margarine.

HEALTH BREAD-MIX

This comes in a packet and is usually a mixture of wholemeal flour, soya flour, sea salt and a little demerara sugar. The right amount of dried yeast is supplied. Follow instructions for mixing and rising and bake in the Multi Cooker as suggested in directions for bread on p. 161.

To thaw frozen bread or rolls: Place on rack in Cooker. Turn heat to 420 (6). Allow about 10 minutes for bread, 5 minutes for rolls.

SWEET YEAST DOUGH FOR BUNS
AND TEACAKES

as an oven   makes a 7 in (17·5 cm) teacake and 9 large sultana buns

Once bitten by the yeast-cooking bug, one is tempted to have a go at the whole range. Sweet yeast dough is one important branch and may be used in many interesting ways.

2 oz (50 g) butter or margarine
1 oz (25 g) caked yeast or ½ oz
  (13 g) dried yeast
4 oz (100 g) sugar
¼ pint (150 ml) warm water
¼ pint (150 ml) cold milk

1 large egg, beaten
1 lb (½ kg) plain flour
4 oz (100 g) cornflour
2 level teaspoons salt
about 6 oz (175 g) sultanas
1 teaspoon vanilla flavouring

1 Put butter or margarine in a small saucepan and begin to melt very gently.
2 If using caked yeast, put it in a cup with 1 teaspoon of the sugar and stir until a liquid is formed, then add the warm water. If using dried yeast, put it in a cup with 1 teaspoon of the sugar and the warm water. Allow both to froth.
3 When fat has melted remove from heat and stir in the milk, then add the yeast mixture and the egg.
4 Sieve together into a large mixing bowl the flour, cornflour and salt.
5 Add the rest of the sugar and the sultanas to the flour mixture.
6 Add vanilla to yeast liquid then stir into the flour mixture. Form into a soft dough. Put rack into Cooker and place mixing bowl on it. Turn control slowly from the 'off' position and when light comes on, stop and leave it there. Cover bowl with a cloth or foil, then cover with Cooker lid. Close vent. Leave to rise for about 2 hours or until doubled in bulk.
7 Lift out and tip dough on to a floured surface. Knead for about 3 or 4 minutes. The dough is now ready to be used. See following recipes.

SULTANA BUNS

1 Follow Sweet Yeast Dough recipe (*p. 163*) and at step 7 leave the heat on in the Cooker. After kneading the dough, break off pieces the size of golf balls and with floury hands roll into balls.

2 Use a tray or shallow cake tin or a folded piece of foil. Grease well. Place on rack in Cooker and put buns on it about ¾ in (2 cm) apart. They should join together after rising. Cover with Cooker lid and close vent. Allow to rise until rolls have increased by half, about 1 hour.

3 Turn to 420 (6) and allow 25–30 minutes. While still hot, brush with Bun Wash (*see below*).

HOT CROSS BUNS

1 Follow Sweet Yeast Dough recipe (*p. 163*). At step 4 add 2 level teaspoons mixed spice and ½ teaspoon nutmeg. Omit sultanas.

2 Proceed then as for Sultana Buns above. After placing the buns on the tray or foil, make two indentations with a knife to form a cross. After cooking, brush with Bun Wash (*see below*), then ice the cross with white icing.

YEAST TEACAKE

1 Follow Sweet Yeast Dough recipe (*p. 163*), but omit sultanas. The quantity will make two 7 in (17·5 cm) teacakes, so half the dough could be put away in the refrigerator for use later.

2 Pat or roll out the remaining half of the dough into a 7 in (17·5 cm) round, about 1 in (2·5 cm) thick. Place in tin and with a knife cut into segments radiating from the centre. Proceed then with the rising and cooking as for Sultana Buns above. While still hot, brush with Bun Wash (*see below*).

Bun Wash: Boil together for 2 minutes 2 rounded tablespoons sugar with 1 tablespoon water. Brush buns with this while they are still hot to make them shine.

DUSKY YEAST POPOVERS

These are made with a batter rather than a dough and therefore have a different texture from the usual bread roll. They are impressive when served hot as part of a lunch menu.

1 tablespoon butter or margarine	*2 teaspoons dark brown sugar*
¼ pint (150 ml) cold milk	*½ lb (225 g) plain flour*
¼ pint (150 ml) hot water	*1½ oz (38 g) cornflour*
2 beef stock cubes	*½ level teaspoon salt*
½ oz (13 g) caked yeast	
or ¼ oz (7 g) dried yeast	

1 Melt butter or margarine in a small saucepan. Remove from heat and add the milk and water. Stir in the crumbled stock cubes.
2 If using caked yeast, mix it in a cup with the sugar until it forms a liquid. If using dried yeast, put it in a cup with the sugar and 2 tablespoons of the warm mixture. Allow to stand for 10 minutes or until it begins to froth, then stir into butter and liquid mixture.
3 Sieve flour, cornflour and salt into a mixing bowl. Make a well in the centre and pour in the liquid. Stir until a thick pliable batter is formed. Beat for about 3 minutes with a wooden spoon.
4 Put rack into Cooker and place bowl on it. Cover with a cloth or foil. Turn control from 'off' position slowly until light comes on. Leave it there. Cover with lid and close vent. Leave for about 2 hours, or until batter has doubled in bulk.
5 Meanwhile, grease well 12 pattypans or foil baking cases.
6 Remove batter from Cooker and leave heat on. Beat again for 3 minutes. Fill pattypans two-thirds full and put back into Cooker. Cover with lid and leave to rise for about 45 minutes, or until risen almost to the top of the pans. Then turn heat to 420 (6) and open vent. Allow 20–25 minutes. Serve hot. To heat and freshen next day, or later, see Note, p. 168.

BREAD-STRIKE LOAF

as an oven   *makes a 1 lb (½ kg) loaf*

When a bread strike descends and there's no time to tackle the yeast routine, a baking-powder loaf can be quickly mixed and baked. Soda bread, traditional to many parts of the British Isles, is made in the same way, except that the two components of baking powder, soda and cream of tartar, are added separately. Double quantities for a large 2 lb (1 kg) loaf.

¾ lb (350 g) self-raising flour
1 level teaspoon baking powder
1 level teaspoon salt
2 tablespoons butter or margarine

2 teaspoons sugar
¼ pint (150 ml) milk, or half milk
and half water

1 Put rack in Cooker and heat to 420 (6).
2 Use a 1 lb (½ kg) loaf tin. For double quantity use either a 2 lb (1 kg) loaf tin or two 1 lb (½ kg) tins. Freezer foil containers are available in both sizes. If tin is not non-stick, grease well. (Foil is non-stick.)
3 Sieve flour, baking powder and salt into mixing bowl. Rub the fat in lightly with fingertips to the consistency of breadcrumbs. Add sugar.
4 Stir in the liquid and mix to a slightly wet dough, adding a little more liquid if necessary. Put into loaf tin and place on rack. Cover with Cooker lid and open vent. Allow 35–40 minutes for a 1 lb (½ kg) loaf, 1¼ hours for a 2 lb (1 kg) loaf. Try not to look until 10 minutes before cooking time is up.

Wholemeal bread-strike loaf: Use half wholemeal and half white flour, or any proportion you wish. Use brown sugar.

Bran bread-strike loaf: Replace 2 oz (50 g) white flour with 1½ oz (38 g) fresh milled bran. Use brown sugar. Wheatgerm could also be added.

Cheese bread-strike loaf: To main recipe or any of the variations, add 3–4 oz (75–100 g) grated Cheddar or Parmesan cheese. Season with pepper and omit sugar.

BAKING POWDER MUFFINS

These American-style muffins are similar to cup cakes, but not so sweet. They are the perfect accompaniment to morning coffee, especially when guests are expected. They should be served hot, split and buttered.

*1 rounded tablespoon margarine
  or butter
2 tablespoons golden syrup
6 oz (175 g) self-raising flour
½ teaspoon salt*

*1 egg
¼ pint (150 ml) milk
½ level teaspoon bicarbonate of
  soda
½ teaspoon vanilla flavouring*

1 Put rack in Cooker and heat to 420 (6).
2 Use 12 deep pattypans or foil baking cases, and brush with a little melted margarine.
3 Melt the butter or margarine with the golden syrup in a small saucepan.
4 Sieve flour and salt into a mixing bowl.
5 Beat egg, then add milk and soda. Stir until soda has dissolved completely. Add vanilla.
6 Add liquid to flour with the melted mixture. Stir moderately. If there are lumps, don't worry, they will disappear during cooking.
7 Put a good tablespoon of the mixture into each pattypan. Place on rack, cover with Cooker lid and open vent. Allow 20 minutes.

Note: To reheat—place on rack in Cooker and turn heat to 420 (6). Cover with Cooker lid and close vent. Allow about 8 minutes.

Ginger muffins: Add 1 good teaspoon ground ginger and ¼ teaspoon nutmeg.

Sultana muffins: Add 2–3 oz (50–75 g) sultanas.

Walnut and date muffins: Add 1½ oz (38 g) chopped walnuts and 2 oz (50 g) chopped, stoned dates.

Cheese muffins: Add 2–3 oz (50–75 g) grated tasty cheese and increase salt to 1 teaspoon. Add a little pepper. Replace golden syrup with 2 tablespoons water and 1 teaspoon sugar.

BRAN HEALTH MUFFINS

With this combination of ingredients, a bran muffin a day must surely keep the doctor away!

3 oz (75 g) plain milled bran (not proprietary processed bran)
4 oz (100 g) self-raising flour
1 level teaspoon salt
2 tablespoons oil or 1 rounded tablespoon butter or margarine

3 tablespoons molasses, or 2 tablespoons treacle and 1 tablespoon golden syrup
1 level teaspoon bicarbonate of soda
¼ pint (150 ml) milk

1 Put rack in Cooker and heat to 420 (6). Grease with oil or butter 12 deep pattypans or muffin pans, or foil baking cases.
2 Put bran, sifted flour and salt into a mixing bowl.
3 In a small saucepan melt the butter or margarine and the syrup, or combine the oil and the syrup.
4 Stir the soda into the milk and let it dissolve.
5 Pour into the dry ingredients with the melted mixture. Mix well.
6 Drop a tablespoon of the mixture into each pattypan.
7 Put rack into Cooker and place pans on it. Cover with Cooker lid and close vent. Cook for 18 minutes.

Note: To freshen stale muffins—preheat Cooker to 420 (6) and put them on the rack. Cover with Cooker lid with vent open and allow about 3 minutes.

YOGHURT DOUGHNUTS

Doughnuts should be eaten warm. Those that are not eaten straight away may be reheated the next day or after freezing. The Cooker is ideal for such a job (*see Note below*).

for frying: ½ litre (500 ml) corn or
  vegetable oil, or 1 lb other
  frying fat
8 oz (225 g) self-raising flour
½ teaspoon baking powder
1 level teaspoon salt

1 oz (25 g) butter or margarine
1 rounded teaspoon sugar
1 egg, beaten
½ carton natural yoghurt (about
  2½ fl oz or 75 ml)
icing sugar

1 Put frying fat into Cooker and set heat at 300 (3).
2 Sift flour, baking powder and salt and rub in the butter or margarine until mixture is crumbly. This may be done in the electric mixer. Add sugar.
3 Add egg and yoghurt and mix to a soft dough. Roll out to ½ in (1·25 cm) thickness.
4 Raise Cooker heat to 340 (4).
5 Cut dough with a 3 in (7·5 cm) cutter (or a cup would do) and cut a 1 in (2·5 cm) round piece from the centres with a 1 in (2·5 cm) cutter or anything else of a suitable size, such as the screw-top of a fruit squash bottle.
6 When light goes out, fry the doughnuts until lightly browned on both sides, about 4–5 minutes altogether. Lift on to dull brown paper, preferably, or kitchen paper and dust with icing sugar. Eat with jam or honey.

Note: To reheat—put rack into Cooker, turn to 420 (6) and after 5 minutes put doughnuts on rack. Heat until soft and moist, about 3 minutes.

Scones of Many Kinds

You won't find Mrs Beeton suggesting frivolous variations to her good plain scones. It was probably the Americans who thought up such an array; and not only that: they called them 'biscuits'! In fact this is not as odd as it sounds. Something like a scone was made in Europe in the eighteenth century and was called a 'Savoy biscuit'. This may have emigrated, retaining its name. The recipe below is a time-saver: using oil instead of butter saves all that rubbing-in.

PLAIN SCONES

8 oz (225 g) self-raising flour
¼ teaspoon salt
¼ level teaspoon baking powder
2 teaspoons sugar
¼ pint (150 ml) milk

2 tablespoons corn or soya bean oil
beaten egg or evaporated milk (optional)

1 Put rack in Cooker and heat to 420 (6). Put a 9 in (22·5 cm) square of foil on top of rack.
2 Sieve the flour into a mixing bowl with the salt and the baking powder. Add the sugar.
3 Add the oil to the milk. Pour into dry ingredients and mix lightly into a soft dough.
4 Pat out to about ¾ in (2 cm) thickness and cut into rounds or squares. The tops may be brushed with beaten egg or evaporated milk.
5 Place on the foil, cover with lid and open vent. Allow about 9 minutes on one side, then turn over and allow 5–6 minutes on the other side.

Wholemeal scones: Replace half the flour with wholemeal flour and increase baking powder to 1 level teaspoon.

Yoghurt scones: Replace milk with yoghurt.

Sultana cinnamon scones: To the dry ingredients add 1 good teaspoon cinnamon and 3 oz (75 g) sultanas. Increase sugar to 3 teaspoons.

Coffee and walnut scones: Add 1 heaped teaspoon ground instant coffee and $1\frac{1}{2}$ oz (38 g) chopped walnuts to the dry ingredients; $\frac{1}{2}$ teaspoon mixed spice could be added.

Butterscotch pinwheels: Make either plain scones or any of the above variations and roll dough into a long strip $6\frac{1}{2}$ in (16·25 cm) wide and $\frac{1}{2}$ in (1·25 cm) thick. Spread with soft margarine, then sprinkle generously with dark soft brown sugar. A little cinnamon may be added. Roll from long side into a long roll and pinch edge to seal. Cut into 1 in (2·5 cm) pieces. Have Cooker heat at 380 (5) and brush foil with oil or melted butter or margarine. When light goes out, put scones on to the foil cut sides up. Cook for 8–9 minutes on one side with vent open, then turn over and cook for 5 minutes on the other side.

Cheese scones: To the dry ingredients add 2 oz (50 g) grated tasty cheese, 1 crumbled chicken stock cube and a little pepper. Monosodium glutamate or seasoning salt may be added.

Cheese pinwheels: Make Cheese Scone mixture. Roll into a long strip as for Butterscotch Pinwheels. Spread with soft margarine then sprinkle generously with grated cheese, using about 4 oz (100 g). Sprinkle with salt and pepper and a little monosodium glutamate or seasoning salt. A different flavour may be achieved by mixing the grated cheese with 1 level dessertspoon of packet tomato-soup-mix plus 1 teaspoon sugar. Roll from long side into a long roll and cut into 1 in (2·5 cm) pieces. Brush foil with oil or melted margarine or butter. Have heat at 380 (5) and when light goes out, put scones on the foil, cut sides up. Cover with Cooker lid and open vent. Cook for 8–9 minutes on one side, then turn over and cook for 5 minutes on the other side.

SCOTCH PANCAKES, OR 'PIKELETS'

as a frypan or as a griddle   *makes 18–20*

Today the teatime Scotch pancakes of Britain are exactly the same as the pikelets of New Zealand and Australia. But this was not always so. English pikelets were once made with yeast and were similar to a crumpet. In the mid-nineteenth century, when the pioneers went out to the new colonies, they took with them the name pikelet, but, when making them, replaced the yeast with soda and cream of tartar (or baking powder). Today, self-raising flour is used. The name Scotch pancake evolved differently. It was once called a Scotch crumpet, and is described in an old Scots cookery book as more of a small pancake than a crumpet. In other words, like a pikelet!

1 egg	*1 tablespoon corn oil or other*
1 level tablespoon sugar	*cooking oil*
4 oz (100 g) self-raising flour	*4 tablespoons milk*
¼ teaspoon salt	*2 tablespoons water*

1 Beat together the egg and sugar until light and frothy. Sieve in flour and salt then add oil and liquid. Beat well (*see Note*).
2 Melt about 2 teaspoons of butter (or use oil) in Cooker with heat at 340 (4) and brush fat well over surface.
3 When light goes out, drop mixture from the end of a dessertspoon to form flat cakes about 3 in (7·5 cm) in diameter. When bubbles appear on the top and they are golden brown underneath flip over and cook on the other side. Cook 3 or 4 at a time.
4 Brush Cooker again with fat and repeat with 3 or 4 more. Continue until all the batter is used up. Eat fresh, spread with butter.

Note: The ingredients may be whisked together in the blender, but it is easier to use the mixture from a bowl.

APPLE TEATIME LOAF

There's a lovely fresh flavour of apple and spice in this loaf. The quantity is for a smaller-sized loaf tin but, if wished, double the quantity and use a large 2 lb (1 kg) tin, or two smaller ones. The two sizes are available in freezer foil containers.

6 oz (175 g) self-raising flour
$\frac{1}{2}$ level teaspoon baking powder
$\frac{1}{2}$ teaspoon salt
$1\frac{1}{2}$ oz (38 g) butter or margarine
2 oz (50 g) light brown sugar
1 eating apple, about 4 oz (100 g)
2 teaspoons sugar

$\frac{1}{2}$ teaspoon ground cinnamon
2 tablespoons lemon juice, with grated rind if you are using fresh lemons
4 tablespoons milk or yoghurt
chopped walnuts or sultanas (optional)

1 Use a 1 lb ($\frac{1}{2}$ kg) loaf tin (metal or freezer foil), and grease well if it is not non-stick.
2 Put rack in Cooker and heat to 420 (6).
3 Sieve flour, baking powder and salt into a mixing bowl.
4 Rub in the butter or margarine then add sugar.
5 The peeled, cored apple may be chopped and mashed in the blender, or stewed, with the sugar and lemon juice. Add cinnamon.
6 Stir into dry ingredients and mix to a sticky dough with the milk or yoghurt. Add walnuts or sultanas, if used. Put into loaf tin and place on rack. Cover with Cooker lid and open vent. Reduce heat to 380 (5) and cook for 40–45 minutes.
7 Cool for about 15 minutes, then turn out. Serve sliced and buttered.

Pineapple teatime loaf: Follow above recipe, using 3 rings of pineapple (5 oz, 150 g), either finely chopped or mashed in blender, with 2 tablespoons yoghurt or cream. Use only 2 tablespoons milk. Omit cinnamon and add the lemon juice.

CHOCOLATE DATE SHORTCAKE

makes an 8 in (20 cm) tart

Mashed dates flavoured with lemon juice are cooked between two layers of chocolate shortcake. This may be eaten either as a cake or as a pudding.

4 oz (100 g) butter or margarine
4 oz (100 g) dark brown sugar
1 dessertspoon hot water
8 oz (225 g) self-raising flour
1 level dessertspoon cocoa
½ teaspoon salt
1 egg
1 teaspoon vanilla flavouring

walnuts for topping
icing sugar

FILLING

4 oz (100 g) dates, stoned
4 tablespoons lemon juice
1 rounded tablespoon brown sugar

1 Cream the fat, sugar and hot water, either in electric mixer or by hand.
2 In a small saucepan cook together until just boiling, the dates, lemon and sugar. Draw off the heat and mash.
3 Use an 8 in (20 cm) square or round cake tin about 1¼–1½ in (3.5 cm) deep.
4 Put rack in Cooker and heat to 420 (6).
5 Sieve together the flour, cocoa and salt.
6 Add 1 dessertspoon of the dry ingredients to the creamed mixture, then the unbeaten egg. Add vanilla flavouring. Beat well.
7 Sieve in the rest of the dry ingredients and work into a dough.
8 Divide in half and roll out one piece to fit the tin. Line bottom of tin with it and neaten edges. Spread with the date mixture.
9 Roll out the other piece and fit on top of the dates. Pinch edges to decorate, then top with a few quartered walnuts.
10 Place on rack. Cover with Cooker lid and open vent. After 5 minutes reduce heat to 380 (5). Allow 40–45 minutes. Do not look until 40 minutes are up. Lift out and put on to a rack. Leave until nearly cold then turn out. Dust with icing sugar.

ALMOND FEATHER CAKE

The extra lightness that characterizes this cake depends on the addition at the end of the stiffly beaten egg whites. A little more trouble but worth it.

4 oz (100 g) butter or margarine
4 oz (100 g) sugar
1 tablespoon boiling or very hot water
5 oz (150 g) self-raising flour plus ¼ level teaspoon baking powder
¼ teaspoon salt

2 large eggs
2 rounded tablespoons ground almonds
¼ teaspoon each of almond and vanilla flavouring
2 tablespoons milk
2 tablespoons water

1 Put butter, sugar and hot water into mixing bowl and begin to cream.
2 Put rack in Cooker and heat to 420 (6).
3 Use a 7 in (17·5 cm) cake tin about 2½ in (6·25 cm) deep. If not non-stick, grease the sides and put a piece of butter or margarine paper on the bottom.
4 Continue creaming until smooth.
5 Sieve together the flour, baking powder and salt. Add 1 dessert-spoon of it to the creamed mixture.
6 Separate the eggs, dropping the whites into a bowl and the yolks into the creamed mixture. Beat well.
7 Add half the flour to the mixture, then the almonds and flavourings. Add milk, then the rest of the flour. Mix, then add water.
8 Lastly beat the egg whites until stiff and fold in. Do not beat again. Tip into cake tin, smooth the top and place on rack. Cover with Cooker lid and open vent. Reduce heat to 380 (5) and cook for 1 hour 5 minutes. Press top lightly with the finger and if it springs back the cake is done. If not, allow another 5 minutes. Try not to look before 1 hour is up.

Note: The top will not be quite as brown as oven-cooked cakes, but if it is iced with Creamy Icing (*p. 194*) and decorated with blanched, sliced almonds, it will look just as smart.

HAZELNUT NUTTY NUT-CAKE

as an oven

In the days when hazelnuts cost something around two shillings a pound, a large cake could be made using all hazelnuts, leaving hardly a dent in the housekeeping. Ways of economizing are possible and these are suggested below. All are nuttier than the usual nut-cake.

8 oz (225 g) hazelnuts	2 large eggs
1 level teaspoon baking powder	½ teaspoon salt
4 oz (100 g) brown sugar	½ teaspoon vanilla flavouring

1 Mince the hazelnuts or grind in blender. Do not grind to a powder —they should be gritty. Add baking powder.
2 Use an 8 in (20 cm) sponge cake tin and if not non-stick, grease sides well and put a piece of butter or margarine paper on the bottom.
3 Put rack in Cooker and heat to 420 (6).
4 Beat the sugar and eggs together until frothy and smooth. Add salt and vanilla flavouring.
5 Stir into nuts and mix well. Pour into tin and place on rack in Cooker. Cover with lid and open vent.
6 Reduce heat to 380 (5) and cook for about 40 minutes.
7 Cool, then turn out and ice with Mocha Icing (*p. 194*).

Hazelnut nutty nut-cake with biscuit crumbs: Use 4 oz (100 g) hazelnuts and 3 oz (75 g) crushed digestive biscuits. Reduce sugar to 3 oz (75 g).

Peanut nutty nut-cake: Replace the hazelnuts with unsalted peanuts.

Walnut nutty nut-cake: Replace the hazelnuts with finely chopped walnuts, or combine half walnuts with half hazelnuts or peanuts.

DEVIL'S FOOD CAKE

as an oven

A moist rich chocolate cake, darkly sinister!

6 tablespoons milk
2 oz (50 g) dark chocolate, broken into pieces
¼ level teaspoon bicarbonate of soda
4 oz (100 g) butter or margarine

5 oz (150 g) brown sugar
8 oz (225 g) self-raising flour
½ teaspoon salt
1 level dessertspoon cocoa
3 large eggs
1 teaspoon vanilla flavouring

1 Use an 8 in (20 cm) round or square cake tin about 2½ in (6·25 cm) deep. If not non-stick, grease sides and put margarine or butter paper on the bottom.
2 Heat milk and chocolate in a small saucepan but do not boil. Let chocolate melt. Add the soda and stir well.
3 Put rack in Cooker and heat to 380 (5).
4 Put 1 tablespoon of the hot chocolate mixture into mixing bowl and add fat and sugar. Beat until smooth.
5 Sieve together the flour, salt and cocoa. Add 1 dessertspoon of this to the creamed mixture then add 1 egg. Beat this in, then repeat with the other two eggs. Beat well.
6 Sieve in the rest of the dry ingredients alternating with the rest of the chocolate mixture. Add vanilla.
7 Tip into tin and smooth top evenly. Place on rack, cover with Cooker lid and open vent. Allow 1 hour 10 minutes. Try not to look until 5 minutes before the end.
8 Ice with Chocolate or Mocha Icing (*p. 194*).

DATE AND CANDIED PEEL CAKE

as an oven

A quickly mixed, moist cake with a spicy, 'more-ish' flavour.

4 oz (100 g) dates, stoned
2 oz (50 g) mixed candied peel, chopped
4 tablespoons boiling water
4 oz (100 g) butter or margarine
4 oz (100 g) soft brown sugar
6 oz (175 g) self-raising flour
¼ teaspoon salt
¼ teaspoon cinnamon

¼ teaspoon nutmeg
1 rounded teaspoon cocoa
2 large eggs
1 teaspoon vanilla flavouring
2 tablespoons milk
1–2 oz (25–50 g) walnuts, chopped (optional)
2–3 oz (50–75 g) sultanas (optional)

1 Put chopped dates, candied peel and boiling water into mixing bowl. Allow to stand for about 5 minutes.

2 Use an 8 in (20 cm) tin about 2 in (5 cm) deep. If not non-stick, grease sides well and put a piece of butter or margarine paper on the bottom.

3 Put rack in Cooker and heat to 420 (6).

4 Add fat and sugar to date mixture and beat until creamy. The warmth of the date mixture hastens this.

5 Sift together the flour, salt, spices and cocoa and add 1 dessertspoon of it to the creamed mixture. Stir, then add one of the eggs. Beat well, then repeat with another dessertspoon of the dry ingredients and the second egg. Beat well.

6 Add the rest of the dry ingredients with the vanilla flavouring and milk. Stir. Add walnuts and sultanas, if used.

7 Pour into cake tin and smooth the top evenly. Place on rack, cover with Cooker lid and open vent. Reduce heat to 380 (5) and allow 1 hour 5 minutes or until cooked.

8 When cooked remove to a cake rack and stand for 5–10 minutes before turning out. Ice with Chocolate Icing (*p. 194*).

MADEIRA CAKE

as an oven

With a basic recipe, many Madeira Cake variations may be made using the Cooker—good news for those in small flats with no oven.

6 oz (175 g) butter or margarine
6 oz (175 g) sugar
1 tablespoon golden syrup
1 tablespoon hot water
7 oz (200 g) self-raising flour

¼ teaspoon salt
3 eggs
1 teaspoon vanilla flavouring
3 tablespoons milk and water,
   half and half

1 Use an 8 in (20 cm) cake tin about 2½ in (6·25 cm) deep. If not non-stick, grease sides well and put butter or margarine papers on the bottom.

2 Cream the fat, sugar, golden syrup and water together, either with electric mixer or by hand.

3 Put rack in Cooker and heat to 420 (6).

4 Sieve together the flour and salt. Add 1 dessertspoon of this to the creamed mixture. Mix, then drop in one of the eggs and beat well. Repeat with the other two eggs. Beat well. Add vanilla flavouring.

5 Add the rest of the flour alternately with the milk. Stir until well blended, but do not beat.

6 Tip into cake tin and smooth the top. Place on rack, cover with Cooker lid and open vent. Reduce heat to 380 (5) and allow 1 hour 10 minutes. Try not to look until 5 minutes before the end.

Coconut Madeira cake: Use 6 oz (175 g) flour and add 1 oz (25 g) desiccated coconut.

Chocolate cake: Replace ½ oz (13 g) of the flour with cocoa or cooking chocolate. Coconut could also be added, as above.

ONE-EGG FRUIT CAKE

as an oven

A basic cut-and-come-again cake. Quantities for a larger cake are given below.

4 oz (100 g) butter or margarine
4 oz (100 g) soft brown sugar
1 dessertspoon golden syrup
6 oz (175 g) self-raising flour
¼ teaspoon salt
1 rounded teaspoon cocoa
¼ teaspoon mixed spice

1 egg
4 oz (100 g) sultanas or mixed dried fruit
¼ teaspoon each of vanilla, lemon and almond essence
4 tablespoons milk

1 Put rack in Cooker and heat to 420 (6).
2 Use a 6–6½ in (16 cm) diameter deep cake tin and if not non-stick, grease sides well and put butter or margarine papers on the bottom.
3 Cream together the fat, sugar and golden syrup.
4 Sift together the flour, salt, cocoa and spice. Add 1 dessertspoon of this to the creamed mixture.
5 Add the egg and beat well.
6 Add the rest of the dry ingredients, then the fruit, essences and milk. Mix well, then tip into tin and spread evenly.
7 Put into Cooker, cover with lid and open vent. Reduce heat to 380 (5) and allow 1½ hours. Try not to look before the last 5 minutes. Leave in the cake tin for about 30 minutes or longer before turning out.

Larger size: For a 7–7½ in (18·5 cm) cake tin increase quantities thus: 6 oz (175 g) butter or margarine; 6 oz (175 g) sugar; 1 level tablespoon golden syrup; 8 oz (225 g) flour; 1 heaped teaspoon cocoa; ¾ teaspoon mixed spice; 2 eggs; 6 oz (175 g) dried fruit; ¾ teaspoon essences; 6 tablespoons milk. Bake for an extra 10–15 minutes.

THREE-MINUTE SPONGE

as an oven

Many years ago, I saw a recipe which said: 'Beat for 2 minutes on electric mixer, or 300 strokes by hand.' So, as I was not looking for such punishment, I bought myself a mixer.

Oil saves time too but use melted butter if you prefer it.

2 large eggs	1 level tablespoon cornflour
5 oz (150 g) sugar	1 level teaspoon baking powder
2 tablespoons oil or melted butter	½ teaspoon salt
(use corn oil or soya bean oil)	3 tablespoons water
4 oz (100 g) self-raising flour	½ teaspoon vanilla flavouring

1 Put rack in Cooker and heat to 420 (6).
2 See Note below for sizes of cooking tins. Brush well with oil or melted butter. If non-stick tins are used this will not be necessary.
3 Break eggs into mixing bowl of electric mixer and tip in the sugar. Add oil or melted butter and beat at fast speed for 2 minutes.
4 Sieve in the flour, cornflour, baking powder and salt, then add water and vanilla flavouring. Beat at highest speed for another minute.
5 Tip into tin or tins and place on rack. Cover with lid and open vent. Allow about 25 minutes for the 2 rectangular or 9 in (22·5 cm) square tins, and about 35 minutes for the 8 in (20 cm) tin. The top will not be browned, but this can be disguised with a covering of icing.

Note: Use either a round or square 7½–8 in (19 cm) tin, about 2½ in (6·25 cm) deep, or 2 small freezer foil rectangular ones, 4½ in by 7 in (11·25 cm by 17·5 cm) or a 9 in (22·5 cm) square freezer foil dish.

Fillings and icings: The 7½–8 in (19 cm) cake may be iced with either Rich Plain Icing or Creamy Icing (*p. 194*), any flavour. The two rectangular cakes may be put together with jam and whipped cream or Mock Cream Filling (*p. 194*). The 9 in (22·5 cm) square cake may either be left as it is and iced, or cut in half and treated like the two rectangular ones.

YOGHURT CAKE

Using oil instead of butter or margarine makes this a very quickly mixed cake and the yoghurt gives it a distinctive and attractive flavour. The mixture makes a large cake, but if you would like to make two and put one in the deep freeze, bake in two 1 lb (450 g) loaf tins.

3 large eggs
11 oz (300 g) sugar
5 fl oz (150 ml) natural or fruit yoghurt
5 fl oz (150 ml) of corn or other good cooking oil

11 oz (300 g) self-raising flour
½ teaspoon salt
½ teaspoon almond flavouring

1 Use an 8 in (20 cm) square or round cake tin about 2½ in (6·25 cm) deep, or two 1 lb (450 g) loaf tins. If not non-stick, grease well and line the bottom of the tin with greaseproof paper.
2 Put rack in Cooker and heat to 420 (6).
3 Put eggs and sugar into a large bowl and beat for 2 minutes. Stir in yoghurt, oil and almond flavouring and continue beating until light and bubbly.
4 Sieve in the flour and salt gradually, stirring gently. When well mixed pour into tin or tins and place on rack. Reduce heat to 380 (5) and cover with lid. Open vent.
5 Allow about 1 hour 15 minutes. The smaller cakes should cook in about 1 hour. Try not to look until 5 minutes before time is up. It may be iced; see p. 194.

Chocolate yoghurt cake: To dry ingredients of main recipe add 1 level dessertspoon cocoa or 1 level tablespoon drinking chocolate, and 1 teaspoon vanilla flavouring.

SCOTTISH SHORTBREAD

as an oven   *makes about ¾ lb (350 g)*

This is the basic traditional recipe, half the usual quantity. If you have a family that can't keep away from the cake tins, the Cooker will take the full quantity.

4 oz (100 g) butter, not
  margarine
2 oz (50 g) castor sugar (see
  Note)

4½ oz (113 g) plain flour
2 oz (50 g) cornflour, rice flour
  or ground rice
¼ teaspoon vanilla flavouring

1 Cream butter and sugar together until pale and smooth. This may be done with the electric mixer.
2 Put rack in Cooker and heat to 420 (6). Use a shallow square or rectangular cake tin that will fit into Cooker. Butter it well, unless it is non-stick.
3 Add dry ingredients to creamed mixture and work into a dough. This is best done with a wooden spoon. Add vanilla flavouring.
4 Roll with rolling pin or press by hand to a neat square or rectangular piece a little over ½ in (1.25 cm) thick. This quantity will give a rectangle about 8 in by 6 in (20 cm by 15 cm). Prick all over with a fork, or make other decorative marks. Place in cake tin.
5 Put on rack in Cooker. Lower heat to 340 (4). Cover with Cooker lid and open vent. Cook for 40–45 minutes. Shortbread is always pale. In the Cooker it will be lightly browned underneath.
6 Remove from Cooker, cut into fingers while hot, but leave in pan until cold.

Note: If you prefer a sweeter shortbread increase sugar to 2½ or 3 oz (63–75 g).

Petticoat tails: So-called (they say) because of the tiny waist in the middle and the flared 'skirt' radiating from it. Put the rolled or pressed-out dough into a 7 in (17.5 cm) shallow cake tin. Pinch around edge to decorate. With a 1½–1¾ in (4 cm) biscuit cutter, cut a round in the middle, then cut segments radiating from it. Prick with a fork or decorate with another utensil (for instance the end of a potato piping nozzle). Bake as for Scottish Shortbread.

GOLDEN-TOP APPLE TURNOVERS

The evaporated milk combines with the cinnamon and sugar to give the popular apple turnover its golden top. Ideal for picnics and packed lunches.

about ½ lb (225 g) apples, grated   *evaporated milk*
  or cooked, and sweetened   *castor sugar and cinnamon*
½ lb (225 g) short pastry (p. 193)
  or use bought pastry

1 Have apple and pastry prepared.
2 Put rack in Cooker and heat to 420 (6).
3 Roll out pastry a little less than ¼ in (0·5 cm) thick and cut into rounds with a 4 or 4½ in (10·5 cm) cutter (or use something round, such as the lid of a biscuit tin).
4 Put a good teaspoon of the apple on one half of each round and fold over, into a half-moon shape. Seal edges with a fork. Brush over with evaporated milk and sprinkle with a mixture of castor sugar and cinnamon.
5 Place either a greased shallow cake tin or a smooth piece of foil on the rack and arrange the turnovers on it. Cover with Cooker lid and open vent. Allow 20–25 minutes.

VARIATIONS

Apple and sultana turnovers: Add about 2 oz (50 g) sultanas to the apple.

Date and walnut turnovers: Replace the apple with the following date and walnut mixture. Put 4 oz (100 g) chopped, stoned dates into a saucepan with 3 tablespoons water or lemon juice and 2 teaspoons sugar (4 if lemon has been used). When it comes to the boil remove from heat and mash to a pulp. Add 1 oz (25 g) finely chopped walnuts.

BAKEWELL TART

Traditional English recipes undergo so many changes during the passing years that the originals are often lost. This has happened to the Bakewell Tart. Originally its filling was based on ground almonds. Now cake-crumbs or breadcrumbs are added, and in some recipes the tart is spread with lemon curd instead of traditional raspberry jam. In this recipe the raspberry jam remains, but cake-crumbs are added to replace some of the expensive ground almonds.

6 oz (175 g) bought or homemade short pastry (see p. 193)
about 4 tablespoons raspberry jam
2 oz (50 g) butter
2 tablespoons sugar

1 egg, beaten
2 tablespoons cake-crumbs
2 level tablespoons ground almonds
½ teaspoon almond essence

1 Roll out the short pastry thinly.
2 Put an 8 in (20 cm) square of doubled foil on the bottom of Cooker and heat to 420 (6).
3 Line a shallow 7 in (17·5 cm) cake tin or pie dish with the pastry. Neaten and decorate the edge. Spread with raspberry jam.
4 Cream the butter and sugar, then add the beaten egg, the crumbs, almonds and almond essence. Spread on top of the raspberry jam.
5 Put into Cooker, cover with lid and open vent. Cook for 30–35 minutes.

CHRISTMAS MINCE TART

A wedge of mince pie may not seem like a 'happy month', as an individual pie does, but so much time is saved by making one large one that a recipe might be useful for those who have no time to fiddle.

SHORTCAKE PASTRY
4 oz (100 g) butter or margarine
4 oz (100 g) dark brown sugar
8 oz (225 g) self-raising flour
¼ teaspoon salt
1 egg

FILLING
a 1 lb (½ kg) jar of mincemeat
¼ lb (100 g) extra sultanas or
* raisins or both*
1 teaspoon vanilla flavouring
1 tablespoon sherry or brandy

1 Cream butter and sugar.
2 Sift flour and salt into a bowl. Add 1 dessertspoon of this to the creamed mixture, then drop in the egg and beat well.
3 Add the rest of the flour and form into a dough. Roll out.
4 Put rack in Cooker and heat to 420 (6).
5 Divide dough in half and line a shallow 9 in (23 cm) round or square cake tin.
6 Mix together the ingredients for the filling and spread a layer over the pastry (there could be enough left for another pie). Cover with a layer of pastry, neaten the edge and pinch to decorate. Prick all over with a fork.
7 Place on rack. Cover with Cooker lid and open vent. Turn down to 380 (5) and bake for about 40–45 minutes.

Note: With the left-over pastry, you could make either mince turnovers or small mince pies.

CARAMEL CRISPS

Dusky-coloured biscuits guaranteed to 'bridge that gap' in the nicest possible way.

4 oz (100 g) butter or margarine	1 rounded tablespoon rice flour,
5 oz (150 g) dark soft brown sugar	ground rice, wholemeal flour or cornflour
6 oz (175 g) self-raising flour	1 egg
	1 teaspoon vanilla flavouring

1 Put rack in Cooker and heat to 420 (6).
2 Use a shallow tin, square or rectangular, that will fit into the Cooker. Grease if not non-stick.
3 Cream together the butter and sugar.
4 Sieve the dry ingredients and add 1 dessertspoon to the creamed mixture. Add the egg and beat it well.
5 Add the rest of the dry ingredients and the vanilla flavouring. Mix to a sticky dough.
6 With floury hands form into balls about 1¼ in (3 cm) across. (*See variation below.*) Place on greased tin. Flatten each one with a floury fork.
7 Put tin into Cooker on rack and cover with lid. Open vent. Reduce heat to 380 (5) and cook for 15 minutes.
8 With a palette knife, turn the crisps over and cook for another 5–8 minutes. Allow to cool until just warm and then lift them on to a rack until cold.

Refrigerator biscuits: If you wish to make just half quantity for one batch, form the rest of the dough into a long roll 2 in (5 cm) across and wrap in foil or greaseproof paper. Put into refrigerator (the mixture will last at least 2 weeks) or deep freeze and when needed slice into ¼ in (0·5 cm) biscuits and cook as directed in steps 7 and 8, above.

5

Savoury and Sweet Sauces
Pastry and Crumb Crusts
Icings and Fillings

A short chapter of oddments necessary to most cookbooks.

The quality of most bought frozen or fresh prepared pastry is excellent and those who wish to save time in the kitchen can use it with a clear conscience.

A wide range of proprietary brands of sauces can now be obtained, and although commercial icings and fillings are also available, here the homemade is infinitely preferable.

Savoury Sauces and Gravies

Note: In the following four sauces the flour should be stirred well into the melted fat, and the liquid then stirred in gradually, to ensure a smooth consistency.

BASIC CREAM SAUCE

In a saucepan melt 1 rounded tablespoon (1 oz, 25 g) butter or margarine. When sizzling but not brown, add 1 rounded tablespoon flour. Cook together for 2 minutes, then remove from heat. Whisk in ½ pint (275 ml) milk and return to heat. Cook and stir until thick and smooth. Season with salt and pepper.

Cheese sauce: Add 2–3 oz (50–75 g) grated tasty cheese to Cream Sauce. Season sharply with salt and pepper, and add a little seasoning salt or mustard powder. One teaspoon Worcester sauce, with 1 teaspoon sugar, may also be added.

MUSHROOM SAUCE

For ½ pint (275 ml) sauce, allow 2 oz (50 g) washed, sliced mushrooms. Bacon makes a tasty addition to the sauce. If used, allow ½ rasher, preferably streaky, for this amount of mushrooms. Remove rind and cut into tiny pieces, dropping them into a small saucepan with 1 level teaspoon (½ oz, 13 g) butter. Cook gently for 1 minute then add the mushrooms and continue cooking for 2 minutes. Add 1 level tablespoon flour. Cook together for about 4 minutes until beginning to brown, then remove from heat and add ¼ pint (150 ml) water and ¼ pint (150 ml) milk. Add ½ beef stock cube, crumbled, or 2 teaspoons soy sauce and season with salt and pepper. Return to heat and stir or whisk until smooth and well cooked.

SAUCE ESPAGNOLE

For about ½ pint (275 ml) sauce, allow: 1 oz (25 g) butter and the same of flour; ½ small sliced cleaned carrot; 1 small chopped onion; ½ pint (275 ml) stock (alternatively, water with ½ beef stock cube); 2 cloves of garlic; 1 bay leaf; ½ teaspoon thyme; 2 teaspoons concentrated tomato purée; 1 tablespoon sherry; 1 tablespoon finely chopped ham. Melt the butter in a saucepan, add the carrot, onion, crushed garlic and ham and fry very slowly until onion is golden.

Stir in flour and cook gently until brown. Add liquid, tomato purée, bay leaf and thyme and stir and cook until smooth and thickened. Season well, add 1 teaspoon sugar and simmer gently for about 15 minutes. Remove bay leaf and add sherry before serving.

GRAVY FOR ROAST MEAT

When the meat has been roasted, lift out. Tip Cooker a little and let fat run to one end. Spoon off all but about 1 tablespoon, leaving as much residue as possible. Have Cooker heat at 340 (4). Sprinkle in 1 level tablespoon flour. Cook until browned then reduce heat to 220 (1) and add ½ pint (275 ml) stock or water. If thicker than you like, add more water. If a larger amount of gravy is needed, increase flour to 2 or more level tablespoons and add water in proportion. Season with salt and pepper. If not brown enough add either ½–1 beef stock cube or 2 or 3 teaspoons soy sauce.

Wine gravy: For 'Expensive Steaks' (*p. 74*) only a small amount of gravy is usually needed. Follow above recipe using 1 level dessert-spoon flour, ¼ pint (150 ml) water and 4 tablespoons, or more if liked, red wine or dark sherry. This will enhance the 'supermarket' steaks (*p. 76*).

MINT SAUCE

To 2 good tablespoons finely chopped fresh mint allow 2 tablespoons boiling water, 2 rounded tablespoons sugar and 4 tablespoons vinegar. Pour the boiling water over the mint, then add the other ingredients. Sugar may be adjusted to taste. Season with ½ teaspoon salt and a little pepper.

SAUCES WITH CANNED OR PACKET SOUP-MIXES

When time is short, these soup-sauces may be used. They have the advantage of supplying a great variety of different-flavoured sauces with very little trouble. To ½ pint (275 ml) milk (or other liquid) allow 1 level tablespoon of the packet soup-mix. Canned soups may be used as they are, or diluted with milk or cream, or perhaps wine or sherry.

HOLLANDAISE SAUCE

Here the Multi Cooker may be used as a double-boiler. Pour 2 pints (1¼ litres) water into Cooker and turn to 220 (1). Put 2 beaten egg yolks into a bowl (the sauce will cook more quickly in an enamel or metal bowl than in glass or pottery). Add 3 oz (75 g) softened butter, 2 tablespoons lemon juice, ½ teaspoon sugar and a little salt and pepper. Put bowl into water (which should be boiling) and whisk and cook mixture until thickened. Do not continue cooking once thickened.

TOMATO SAUCE WITH FRESH TOMATOES

Skin ½ lb (225 g) ripe tomatoes. Deseed if liked, but this is not essential. Melt 1 level tablespoon (½ oz, 13 g) butter in a saucepan and add 1 level tablespoon flour. Cook together for 2 minutes without browning. Remove from heat. Add tomatoes, 2 teaspoons brown sugar, 1 tablespoon vinegar, ½ teaspoon basil, and salt and pepper to taste. Return to heat and cook and stir until thick. Thin with a little water or cream.

MAÎTRE D'HÔTEL BUTTER

Use any amount of butter you wish. Soften butter a little; see p. 15 'To soften butter'. For 4 oz (100 g) butter, work in with a knife 1 tablespoon lemon juice and 1 tablespoon finely chopped parsley. If butter is unsalted, add a little salt. Spread out on a plate to about ¼ in (0·5 cm) thickness and put into refrigerator to harden. Cut into 1½ in (3·75 cm) squares and place on cooked steaks or fish just before serving.

Sweet Sauces

LEMON SAUCE FOR PANCAKES

Make Cream Sauce (*p. 189*), without seasoning and using 3 table-spoons less milk. When cooked and thick add the grated rind of a lemon with 3 tablespoons lemon juice.

Quick methods: (1) Dilute lemon honey with water or milk to a thin pouring consistency. (2) Mix together 4 tablespoons sweetened condensed milk with the grated rind and juice of 2 lemons. Dilute with water.

POURING CUSTARD

Here, the Multi Cooker may be used as a double-boiler. Put 2 pints (1¼ litres) water into Cooker and turn heat to 220 (1). Break 1 large egg into an enamel or metal bowl (glass or pottery take longer to heat) and add 1 level dessertspoon sugar and a few drops of vanilla flavouring. Beat well until the white is no longer stringy. Add ½ pint (275 ml) warm milk and stir thoroughly. Place bowl in the boiling water, then stir until custard has thickened and will coat the spoon. When cool it will be thicker.

TO CARAMELIZE CONDENSED MILK FOR CARAMEL SAUCE

Place unopened cans of sweetened condensed milk into a large saucepan or pressure cooker, and cover with water. Put on lid. Boil gently for 3 hours in ordinary saucepan, 1 hour in pressure cooker at 15 lb (7·5 kg) pressure (high). They will keep almost indefinitely. To use, dilute with water or milk.

Caramel rum sauce: Use caramelized condensed milk. Dilute with water and add rum to taste.

Pastry and Crumb Crust

SHORT PASTRY

To make 6 oz (175 g) short pastry, allow 4 oz (100 g) self-raising flour and 2½ oz (63 g) butter or cooking fat (or half and half). Add ¼ teaspoon salt and, for sweet pastry, 2 teaspoons sugar as well. Using finger tips, rub in until mixture resembles fine breadcrumbs; or use an electric mixer. Mix to a firm dough with a little cold water. Roll out.

To make 8 oz (225 g) short pastry, allow 6 oz (175 g) self-raising flour and 3½ oz (88 g) butter or cooking fat (or half and half). Add ½ level teaspoon salt and, for sweet pastry, 3 teaspoons sugar. After rubbing in, mix to a firm dough with a few tablespoons of cold water. Roll out.

PUFF PASTRY

This pastry needs a sudden high heat if it is to puff up the dough into light flaky layers. This can only be done in those Multicookers which have a higher wattage, 1240 or more.

CRUMB CRUST

To line an 8 in (20 cm) flan or pie dish about 1½ in (3·75 cm) deep, allow 6 oz (175 g) crushed biscuits, either all digestive, or part a smooth type of sweet biscuit, 3 oz (75 g) melted butter (not margarine), 2 rounded tablespoons brown sugar, salt, ½ teaspoon vanilla flavouring and 1 egg yolk. If the crust is not to be cooked, replace the egg yolk with an extra rounded dessertspoon butter. Mix together the biscuits, melted butter, sugar, egg yolk (if used), a pinch of salt and vanilla flavouring. Press on to the bottom and sides of the dish. For an uncooked crust put in refrigerator to harden, then neaten the edge.

Black-bottom crumb crust: Follow basic recipe using crushed chocolate biscuits or ginger biscuits.

Icings and Fillings

RICH PLAIN ICING

This has a little butter in it which makes it richer and softer than plain water icing. To 4 oz (100 g) icing sugar, add 1 good teaspoon butter. Add about ¾ tablespoon or more boiling water or lemon juice. Beat well. Will ice an 8 in (20 cm) cake.

Chocolate icing: Add 1 teaspoon cocoa and 1 teaspoon vanilla flavouring.

Coffee icing: Add 1 good teaspoon instant coffee powder and flavour with ½ teaspoon cinnamon and ½ teaspoon vanilla flavouring.

CREAMY CAKE FILLING OR ICING

To 4 oz (100 g) icing sugar add 1 tablespoon butter and about ¾ tablespoon boiling water or lemon juice. Beat until creamy. Will fill an 8 in (20 cm) cake, or may be used as an icing.

Chocolate filling: Add 1 good teaspoon cocoa and flavour with ½ teaspoon cinnamon and ½ teaspoon vanilla flavouring.

Mocha filling: Add 1 level teaspoon instant coffee powder and 1 level teaspoon cocoa. Flavour with ½ teaspoon ground ginger and ½ teaspoon vanilla flavouring.

MOCK CREAM FILLING

Heat ¼ pint (150 ml) milk. Mix 5 level tablespoons cornflour with 1 tablespoon cold water and stir in. Cook and stir until thick and smooth. Remove from heat and cover with lid to prevent a skin forming. Cool. Beat together 1 rounded tablespoon softened butter with 1 rounded tablespoon castor sugar until smooth and creamy. Add ½ teaspoon vanilla flavouring. Beat this into the white sauce until light and creamy. Use in place of whipped cream.

Index

195